# You Ain't Moses

# You Ain't Moses

By LaVerne Thornton

Illustrations by Perry Harrison

CHAPEL HILL
PRESS, INC.

Illustrations by Perry Harrison

Copyright © 2012 LaVerne Thornton

ISBN 978-1-59715-089-7
Library of Congress Catalog Number 2012949524

First Printing

*To Lucille.*

Sharing my life with her for
nearly fifty-six years of marriage
has made me a better man.

FRECKLES

*1997–2012*

Best friend and hiking buddy, for you every day was a new adventure. You were with me on the cover of my first book, but I lost you just as this one was going to press. Fifteen years of your companionship and unconditional love have made my life richer.

*Author's Note*

At this stage of my life, most personal rewards come from helping others and sharing some of what I have learned along the way. One particularly enriching relationship is with Gary Jones, a hard-working, ambitious young man I have the privilege to counsel on business matters. Thank you, Gary, and your wife Imelda, daughter Khaliah, and son Kyle. My work with you to build a business that will support and sustain you and your family in future years keeps me enthusiastic and makes me feel younger than I really am.

# Contents

# Foreword

I first met LaVerne Thornton when he approached me about publishing his first book, *Walk in 'e Moon*, a collection of stories about his childhood growing up in a poor, isolated section of Virginia. I found him to be quietly confident man, soft-spoken, with a dry, slightly racy sense of humor, and an engaging way about him. He was a master storyteller. His writing was both humorous and poignant, resonating with a warmth and appreciation for the important things in life—not money or material things, but friendships and love of family. It took the two of us a while to learn to "read" each other—with his trying his best to get "under my skin" and my often letting him do it—but we laughed often, butted heads some, and always left our meetings in good spirits. Retired for a number of years, LaVerne put his salesman hat back on when the book was released and hit the road, both figuratively and literally, selling an impressive number of copies himself while reconnecting with old friends and meeting new ones.

We stayed in touch after that, with an occasional email or lunch meeting just to catch up on things. I knew he was writing another book—this one a collection of stories about experiences he had as an adult, either in the business world, or as an active retiree—and he would sometimes show me drafts of his new stories. While he has a strong sense of what he wants to say, he welcomes suggestions and observations from others that might help make his writing even better. That trait—a desire to learn from others to make himself more effective—has served him well, not only in business, but also in life.

During the time we have worked together, LaVerne and I have watched each other deal with sadness more than once. The day his first book arrived from the printer, his long-time friend Dave Watson died. (In this book, he writes about their friendship in "Flowers for Dave" and "Helping Dave Die.") LaVerne was visibly shaken at what otherwise would have been a joyous, exciting day. A number of months later, his beloved sister died suddenly, and his correspondence with me reflected his profound grief. Then, in the middle of our work to publish this current book, my mother passed away unexpectedly, and I was sidelined for weeks dealing with the "busyness" and emotion of that loss. I explained what had happened to LaVerne, and he expressed his deep sympathy and understanding. When I got back in touch with him later to resume our work, apologizing for the delay, his response was simple: "Friends are patient with each other."

While his first book is filled with anecdotes about life lessons he learned as a child, often the hard way, this one illustrates how those lessons and core values have served LaVerne—and sometimes given him a wake-up call—in his adult life, as a business and community leader, or simply as a friend. LaVerne Thornton is a keen observer of people. He notices what most others don't, because he experiences interactions with others deeply rather than on the surface as many of us do. In these stories, he tells of being admonished more than once by a boss or colleague for being too soft, getting too personally, emotionally involved in the lives of those who worked for him. In several chapters, he relates experiences in which he inserted himself into the lives of perfect strangers because they needed help in some way. LaVerne cannot live any other way. He relates to people on a human level, regardless of what they do, how they look, how much they have, etc. He finds the humanity in others and never feels superior to another person (unless, of course, it's a Yankee making derisive comments about Southerners).

Working with LaVerne to publish this second book was a labor of love. Whenever we met to discuss editing or design concepts, or to agree on the timetable for work to be completed, he always had a bawdy joke for me, hoping to shock me a little. In addition to talk of the project at hand, we also would compare notes about what was going on in our personal lives, because we genuinely care for each other. I have never been approached by an author to write a foreword, and I hesitated before agreeing to do it for LaVerne. In the end, though, I agreed to do it because I realized I would write this, not as LaVerne Thornton's publisher, but as his friend.

Edwina D. Woodbury

# You Ain't Moses

# Quiet Wisdom

Everything Ernest Wicker owned was clean, square, vertical, plumb and in good working order, including his person. Ernest was about five-feet-seven, with jet-black hair and very dark skin. With his mustache trimmed narrow and turned down a little at the ends of his mouth, he looked like the Mexican banditos we have all seen in Western movies. I think he was mostly Indian.

Ernest worked in the mining department at Pomona Pipe Products. Employees working in the mining department knew they would get dirty at work, so they usually came to work in less-than-pristine condition. Not so Ernest. Ernest arrived at work in clean clothes, clean-shaven, and with that always perfectly trimmed mustache. Although he did a really good, albeit dirty, job, he would leave work looking just as he had looked when he arrived. I eventually learned why. He wore clean clothes to work and brought a full set of work clothes with him. He would shower, wash his hair, and put his clean clothes back on every day before leaving the plant.

Before I became plant manager, the employees had

to park on a muddy hill by the grinding plant. Most of them had to walk a path down a steep bank. This bank was usually ankle-deep in either dust or mud, depending on the weather. Their cars were either muddy or covered by dust just from parking in that lot. The day I became plant manager, I started the work of relocating the parking lot to a flat, well-graveled and graded area that I had already planned to use, just waiting for the day that I was promoted to plant manager. The area was well-drained, very neatly fenced off, and had a gate that opened onto a paved area. This allowed the employees to get to their work area without having to stop and scrape mud from their feet. They could also get in their cars to go home with relatively clean feet. I was thirty years old at the time and did this for the employees strictly from a gut feeling that it would somehow provide an appreciated benefit for them. I was unaware that the real meaning would be interpreted for me by a man who, by his own admission, had attended school only one day in his life. That man was Ernest Wicker.

One day after work, Ernest came to the office and asked to see me. I had made it known to the employees that my door would always be open, so I immediately invited Ernest in. He seemed completely relaxed, probably because I had often stopped to speak to him on the job.

Ernest said, "Mr. Thornton, I want to thank you for the new parking lot." After asking him to call me LaVerne, which he never would, he continued, "I don't have no education. I only went to school one day and never went back. I can't read, but I learn a lot by listening. I heard a preacher explain scripture once about how a good leader is some-body that don't mind serving. He said something about, to be great, you must serve. I've watched you since you got to be the boss. I don't think you are below serving 'cause I heard men who worked for you say that if they have a problem, you will help them with it." Ernest continued, telling how he had asked the previous plant manager if we could get some gravel for the parking lot, but the plant manager had reacted rudely. Ernest went on, "You don't have to prove to the employees that you are better than them; hell, they know that. They just don't like the boss to show it all the time like most plant managers do."

I could hardly speak by now, but I did assure Ernest that I was no better than anyone else. I shook his hand and thanked him for coming in and told him that he was welcome anytime. "If you ever have a problem that I may be able to help you with, you just let me know," I added. This simple man taught me a lesson. I had heard the same scrip-ture before, but had simply learned it by rote. It had never occurred to me that since I had been placed in a position of authority over many people, I could lord it over them. From that day forward I found ways to serve those I had authority over. I never demanded anything from an employee. I asked them, most often with a "please." I can't recall a single time that I received less than enthusiastic cooperation.

I had just been exposed to the best leadership lesson ever, from a man whom the world would call illiterate. I went home and looked up the scripture that Ernest's preacher had referenced. I wanted to learn those verses. I had missed the true meaning of that scripture the other times I heard it. I copied the passage, from the book of Matthew, and kept it in my desk drawer for years.

> Jesus called them together and said, "You know that the rulers of the Gentiles lord it over them, and their high officials exercise authority over them. Not so with you. Instead, whoever wants to become great among you must be your servant, and whoever wants to be first must be your slave—just as the Son of Man did not come to be served, but to serve, and to give his life as a ransom for many." (Matthew 20:25–28, NIV)

I learned more about Ernest as time went by. He was married with no children. He lived in a small, beautiful, modest home just on the edge of Sanford, North Carolina. His yard looked as if he cut his grass with nail clippers. The concrete driveway looked freshly scrubbed. In short, his property looked far better than mine. One day I stopped by where Ernest was working and complimented him on his attractive home. He seemed genuinely proud that I stopped to talk.

He asked, "Do you have anyone to help you with your yard?"

I told him I could handle it alone, but Ernest said he would be glad to help me.

Lo and behold, when I walked out of the house on

Saturday, there was Ernest sitting in his truck. He got out and asked what he could start on.

I asked how much he charged for yard work.

He looked visibly bothered by the question but replied, "Don't pay me anything; just talk to me about things and stuff. I love to learn."

Thus started a long and fruitful relationship with a truly wise man. The other employees kidded Ernest about kissing ass. Ernest told them that he earned more working for me than he had ever earned in his life. He never accepted a dime from me, but I believe our little talks while doing yard work were the earnings he was talking about. We talked about everything. We trimmed shrubs, planted shrubs, and generally groomed my yard to perfection. I was awarded the Yard of the Month by the Goldston Garden Club so many times that I was asked to accept a lifetime award and refrain from entering the monthly contest.

Once while working, I asked Ernest how he had met his wife. He said that one Saturday evening about 6 p.m. he was driving through Cotton Hill, an area east of Sanford where cotton was grown. Cotton Hill was considered a very poor area. Ernest said he had just bought a car and was enjoying a drive through the cottonfields. When passing one field he saw a young girl who looked to be about sixteen years old, chopping cotton.

Ernest said, "I thought to myself, *Any young girl chopping cotton on Saturday afternoon at six o'clock orta make a good wife.* So I stopped and asked her to marry me. She said 'Yes,' and it's worked out real good."

Ernest explained his philosophy of marriage: "I see 'em court for years, marry, and it don't last. I say, find someone you take a liking to, marry her, and learn together how to make it work. I never courted before, and my wife didn't either," said Ernest, "and it sure has worked good."

At the height of the Vietnam War, we used to talk

about the war while we were working in my yard. Being unable to read, Ernest must have developed a keen ability to absorb information by listening, because he had a good command of news details. Eventually during a lull in the conversation he said, "It makes an ignorant man not feel so bad when you see how smart people messed up things like they have in Vietnam." Good point, Ernest!

Ernest had no children. I never asked him about it, and he never told me why. We were talking about children one day while working, and Ernest told me about a shopping trip he went on with his wife to Kmart. Ernest said that he would always stand in one area and wait for his wife to do the shopping. On this night, he told of seeing a woman with a little boy. The mother stood him in one place and in a firm voice said, "You stand there and don't move till I get back." Ernest said that kid never moved from his tracks. Then a woman came in and did about the same thing, but the kid paid her no mind. He was constantly jerking things off counters or running off and having to be retrieved by Mama. Before the lady could pick out what she wanted, both she and the kid were worn to a frazzle.

Ernest said, "That kid that did like his mother told him to knows about everything he will ever know right now. The misbehaving kid left that store having learned a few things." This was comforting to me, when our kids' curiosity would just about kill us.

One Saturday, Ernest and I were working, and the subject of my education came up. I was careful not to boast, but did tell him where I had attended college and what I had studied. He asked a lot of questions. Eventually he said, "I have a cousin that went to Carolina."

"What did he study?" I asked.

"Nothing. They studied him!" I allowed that he is probably a professor there now. With that we both had a belly laugh.

Although our company started a program that encouraged and paid employees to participate in a reading program, Ernest never did. I never spoke with him about it. I decided that Ernest was comfortable with himself. Why mess that up?

A good friend of mine who was an automobile dealer told me he believed he had sold Ernest every car that he ever owned. He always paid cash. One time Ernest picked out a new four-wheel-drive Ford pickup that he really liked. After the usual dickering, they came to an agreed-upon price. Ernest said, "There's just one other thing I have to do. This truck stands taller than the truck I drive now. Can I drive it home and see if my dog can jump into it? He's gettin' a little old."

My friend Welford let Ernest take the truck home for the test. When Ernest returned, Welford asked, "Well, how did it go?"

Ernest said that his dog couldn't jump up into the truck but he was buying it anyway. With a grin he said, "I'm going to make steps for him." Pure Ernest!

I learned from Ernest that wisdom can be acquired without exposure to books.

I learned that lack of education severely limits one's success in life.

I learned that there is something to learn from every human being if you just open up to them.

I learned that one can serve those whom he leads without appearing weak or losing authority over them.

After Ernest visited my office to thank me for the improved parking lot, I made myself available to any employee whom I could help with a problem. They needed help with things like how to apply for a home loan, how to work with contractors and insurance companies if they had a fire, how to apply for Social Security benefits upon retirement, and many other of life's problems employees faced in their daily lives.

I'm a better man for having known Ernest. I said good-bye to Ernest when I left Pomona and told him I would like for our friendship to continue. I went into a different career that kept me away a lot, and our paths eventually separated. I didn't hear of Ernest's death until after he was buried. I was saddened by his passing.

My career travels would often have me going an entire week without meeting any other human whom I had ever before seen. I have, on occasions, relaxed by reflecting on the yard work and conversations Ernest and I had. We sold our company, and I returned to a more routine life. Symbolically speaking, I came home to smell those roses that Ernest and I planted.

Rest in peace, Ernest Wicker. You are unforgettable, my friend.

# Lessons from Mama

My son, my son-in-law, and I arrived at the Grand Canyon on a Thursday in September. We planned to hike from the rim to the bottom and back. I immediately noticed that, although I was breathing very rapidly and vigorously, no oxygen was getting to my lungs. Due to the high elevation, there was no oxygen in the air. I spoke with an eighty-five-year-old man who carried a nail that had been handed down for three generations. The nail had been kept wet for all that time. There had not been enough oxygen in the air to rust that nail for all those years. The first night out, I learned from an old Indian that I should sleep on a pad with my head hanging over the edge of the canyon. This way, an occasional updraft from the bottom of the canyon would bring air up to provide enough oxygen to keep me alive. It was also advised to sleep with my head resting on either a baby diaper or an adult Depends to soak up the nosebleed.

After surviving the night we met the hiking guide by the fireplace in the Bright Angel Lodge, named after the only lying, conniving angel who ever lived. Shane, the guide, was built only of sinew and bone. I immediately noticed that he didn't breathe. He had acclimated to the climate and could live without oxygen. With a sinister grin he explained our hike. He left out all but the fun parts. I interrupted and asked, "Has anyone ever come back?" No answer!

We were driven to the Kaibab trailhead. *Kaibab* is an old Indian word meaning "dumb bastard who think he get back up." At the trailhead, we were given backpacks. The literature had said they would weigh twenty-five pounds, but we passed a truck scale on the way to the trailhead and got an overweight ticket. Each backpack contained twenty-five hundred granola bars, a tent, and enough water to fill a ten-person hot tub. I never slept in my tent, preferring to keep it for use as a burial wrap. It was supposed to be a one-man tent, but the weight made me suspicious. I scratched out a label on it: "Bubba Lamar's healing revival tent."

After strapping on the backpacks we walked to the trailhead. I looked over the rim and saw no bottom. I saw a glow that I took to be the molten core of the earth. The trail was chiseled in the side of a vertical wall and zigzagged down at an angle one degree less than the angle of repose. (The "angle of repose" is that angle that will allow one to stand still without sliding, but if increased by one-tenth of a degree will cause one to slide at the speed of light.) Our backpacks were two inches wider than the trail. This allowed for an occasional bumping of the trail wall that would cast you toward the bottomless abyss. The trail was

constructed of logs anchored across the trail, ostensibly to prevent erosion. The truth is I don't believe they needed to be four feet in diameter. These erosion-prevention devices were placed at a distance apart that would prevent a world-class hiker from ever developing a rhythm.

After about thirty minutes, my heart rate was so fast it could not be counted. My thighs were trembling at three times reggae rhythm. Lactic acid ran out of my muscles and into my shoes. I think this is what caused me to slide over the trail edge to the switchback five feet below. The last thing I remember was seeing Jesus while water was being poured over me. Some said that I begged for Mama and said I was sorry for all the bad I had done. Fortunately I never regained my senses until I was taken to the Phoenix airport. On my next vacation I plan to go over Niagara Falls in a washtub.

Of course, this is a tongue-in-cheek tale that is not totally true, but obviously told for comedic effect. The truth is, I went one mile down into the Grand Canyon, but my better judgment told me that I should turn back, and I did. I was terribly disappointed, ashamed of myself, and felt like a failure. That was at first, but I thought of some lessons I had learned from Mama and took corrective action.

### LESSON ONE

I often went to visit Mama overnight so I could take her to her regular medical checkups. She would always dress really nicely, as if she were going to some fancy place. She arranged her appointments so that we could have lunch in a nice restaurant and go visiting or cruising afterward. Noticing how this routine developed, I asked Mama about it.

Mama explained, "One should provide some sweet with the bitter that life brings to you." With a sly grin she said, "I just don't like going to so many doctors' visits. That is the bitter, and that is why I ask you to do these appointments the way we do. That way, I really look forward to them. That is the sweet. I also want to make it pleasant for you."

Remembering Mama's conversation, what I actually did while the others were hiking was take our rented car and tour the Painted Desert, Lake Powell, and many interesting points on the east end of the Grand Canyon. I was back in time to receive an exhausted, thirsty, and hungry son and son-in-law. I exaggerated with excitement my travels in air-conditioned comfort while they had been suffering in the canyon.

## LESSON TWO

Another lesson that Mama taught me, when I was very young, was that if you feel like a failure at something and it is not a life-or-death matter, find some way to laugh at yourself. I can tell you, it works. I laughed at myself as soon as I started to write this story.

# Servant Leader

A couple of months ago, out of curiosity, I put the title of my first book, *Walk in 'e Moon*, into the Google search engine. After scrolling through all the normal stuff—my website, Amazon.com, and so on—I suddenly saw a posting on a blog by John Lubans. The posting was about my book and Virlie's restaurant in Pittsboro, North Carolina. In it, Lubans described Virlie's as a "great, good place," welcoming and comfortable, where one can pleasantly pass the time. While there, he noticed and bought a copy of my book. I was excited and humbled to read the positive things he had to say about my stories of growing up in a poor, isolated area of Virginia and the life lessons I learned there. I was pleased that someone thought enough of my book to blog about it. I read everything on John's blog (at www.lubans.org). I located his email address and immediately sent him a message. Within a few hours, John replied to my email. I learned that he was, at the time, teaching at the University of Latvia, but his permanent home is in Durham, North Carolina.

I grew up in a small world that, figuratively speaking,

was surrounded by a high wall. I learned early that if I saw
light from the outside world peeking through that wall, I
should squeeze through it and explore a wider world. I saw,
with John's first email, light peeking through that wall.

John and I developed an email friendship that led to a
plan to have lunch at Virlie's when he returned to Durham.
In September 2011 he and I met and enjoyed a delightful

meal at Virlie's. One result of our email friendship was learning that we both were interested in management and leadership. In fact, John is a leadership consultant and has published a book titled *Leading from the Middle*. John asked if I had written anything that would demonstrate my leadership style. I emailed a few stories, and from those John identified me as a "servant leader."

Somehow through my long management career and exposure to numerous management studies, I had missed the term "servant leader," so I went to Google and found this description:

> Servant leadership is a very popular leadership model. It was developed by Robert K. Greenleaf in 1970. The servant leader serves the people he/she leads, which implies that employees are an end in themselves rather than a means to an organizational purpose or bottom line. Servant leadership is meant to replace command and control models of leadership, to be more focused on the needs of others. (Mitch McCrimmon, leadersdirect.com)

That description fit me as comfortably as that Scottish tweed jacket I have had for twenty-four years. Immediately I recalled how and when I had discovered this leadership method as my natural style.

In 1968 I was made plant manager of a plant that manufactured vitrified clay sanitary sewer pipe. I was a tender thirty-one years old at the time. We had about 350 employees. My first act was to build a new parking lot that provided a dignified place for the employees to park their cars. This simple act was so well received that I received many a thank-you.

One day I was walking through the plant and an employee, Donald Yow, asked me if I could give him some advice on a problem. I responded positively, and he explained that, a few months earlier, he and his wife had purchased a new double-wide mobile home. One day his wife had dressed for work and was wearing high-heeled shoes. She stepped into the bathroom for a final mirror check, and one of her heels went right through the vinyl floor. Upon examining the floor, Donald found that the manufacturer had laid the vinyl floor covering over a hole about three inches in diameter. Donald told me that he had tried in vain to get the company to repair the floor, but all he had received was promises. I asked Donald to bring me all the pertinent information, and I said that I would call the company.

The next day Donald brought me a folder with a complete description of the problem and a record of all phone calls he had made in an attempt to get the problem solved. I went back to my office and called the company. Once I reached the right person, explaining who I was and the reason I was calling, the man told me that the company was going to fix the problem.

I replied, "Yes, you are, and you are going to fix it by Friday of this week."

He responded in an arrogant tone.

I said, "If you don't have the repairs done by Friday, a lawsuit will be filed on Monday morning. I will use the full force of our good offices to assist in the suit."

The repairs were made on Thursday.

Word got around the plant quickly. I knew then that I had turned my natural feelings into an effective leadership style that happened to be inconsistent with popular management training concepts during that era. I helped employees with many other things, such as applying for a home mortgage, working with contractors and insurance companies if an employee had a fire, and resolving any number of personal problems. I could feel the respect growing as employee morale and performance, which had been a problem, improved dramatically. The bottom line, as businesspeople like to say, also improved.

I related the mobile-home story to my boss, who had been plant manager ahead of me. His reaction was that I was headed for problems someday if I continued to manage that way. He was an ex-Marine and had served in many bloody battles in the South Pacific during World War II. He brought to the job his habit of shouting, "Take that hill!"—command-and-control leadership.

*Note to that former boss, I am still waiting for those problems you warned me about.*

One of my favorite periods of church life was when our first woman minister, Susan Cafferty, having learned of my background, asked me to serve as a sort of ombudsman for our church. I served as Pastor Parish Relationship chairman through Susan's eleven-year tenure with Goldston United Methodist Church.

As I reflect back on how the servant-leader concept applies so comfortably to me, I have an explanation: as I mentioned, I grew up in a poor, isolated area of Virginia called the Bend. I grew up in a Christian home where my parents and Granny epitomized the expression, "Don't just talk the Christian talk, but walk the Christian walk." The center of our social world was a small country Methodist church built of stone from my family's ancestral land. Our congregation gathered strength and inspiration from each other. Helping each other in our time of need was a shared philosophy. You helped someone simply because they were another human being in need. No college course or book can teach you that.

# You Ain't Moses

A lot is written these days about the drug problem among our youth. I have to admit that I, too, suffered from a drug problem as a boy: I was drug to church. The worst part of that problem was being drug to old-fashioned southern revivals. These revivals were normally held in July in a church building without air conditioning. I had one suit—a wool knickers model. It is not hard to imagine that a boy of eleven could hardly pay attention to those sermons.

That all changed in the summer of my eleventh year on earth. My dad placed a great emphasis on my turning twelve. That age was when I was to magically become a man. Daddy believed that Jesus became a man at twelve years of age when he challenged the elders in the temple.

In the summer of 1948, the countdown year to my turning twelve, we had our revival in July. I realized that becoming a man meant I was to take on a whole new level of attitude and understanding about matters of religion. Try as hard as I might, I could not pay attention to those hellfire-and-brimstone sermons preached by the visiting minister. That all changed prior to the third night of revival. We were having a severe drought that summer. You could observe farmers glaring into the sky constantly looking for any sign of rain. Our crops were drying up in the fields. Gardens that were supposed to provide about all of our food, year-round, were not producing as they should. On our way to revival on a Wednesday night—a day that has left a placeholder in my mind—we had to pass through Calvin's farm. It was pouring down rain there, and it appeared to be raining only on his farm. Now Calvin, based on everything I had ever learned in church, was a heathen, an infidel, and a Class A sinner. Mind you, I was taught not to judge, but I'm just saying that if I were to ever judge someone, this would have been my judgment of Calvin.

That night, the minister used Matthew 5:45 as the scripture for his sermon: "That you may be sons of your Father in heaven. He causes his sun to rise on the evil and the good, and sends rain on the righteous and the unrighteous." My ears perked up, and I was practically struck dumb because for the first time—given my experience on the way to church—I connected a sermon to real life. I saw it raining on the farm of a man who, in my opinion, was unrighteous. I started to listen to sermons and begged forgiveness for all my years of not paying attention.

Listening is not the same as understanding, though, and my listening to sermons got me in trouble.

A few days before I turned twelve, I wrote a poem asking God to help me in the awesome task of becoming a man. I had a vivid imagination. My grandmother,

Shotgun Essie, often called me "My little Solomon." Well, as mothers do, my mother showed my poem to the minister. The minister, probably to humor Mama, asked me to read the poem in church. I could hear my friends teasing, "Pee Wee wrote a poem, Pee Wee wrote a poem."

*God in heaven deliver me from this task!*

No amount of pleading worked. Mama wanted me to read it in church, Daddy wanted me to read it in church, and my minister wanted me to read it. There was no way out.

In our home, after one of us kids turned twelve, Daddy required that we say the blessing at the supper meal. We were required to use our own words and not the standard kids' prayer said by rote. The dreadful date was set for me to read my poem. For dramatic effect, the first Sunday after I turned twelve was chosen.

The last sermon I heard before my appointed day was about the Israelites making a golden calf out of their jewelry so they would have a god to worship. That was while Moses was up on Mount Sinai taking delivery of the Ten Commandments. When Moses came down off the mountain, he and God saw what the people had done. God got so mad at the people that he threatened to destroy them. Moses intervened with God, pleading with Him to spare the people. The minister explained that event as one of the only times he knew of when someone had struck a bargain with God.

At my time to say the blessing at suppertime, I got on a roll. At the end of my blessing, I asked God, "If I read my poem in church Sunday, could you find it possible for

me to have a double-barreled, twenty-gauge shotgun?" When I said "Amen" and glanced up at Daddy, I could see that I had overstepped. All was quiet during the meal. I tried to come up with an escape mechanism, but decided that whatever was coming wouldn't be good, so I may as well face it and put it behind me as soon as possible.

After we finished eating, Daddy stared that powerful stare and said to me, "I don't want to ever hear you bargain with God again." He said it with such force that nothing else needed to be said. I don't know to this day what prompted me, but I blurted out, "Moses bargained with God!" Daddy stared again and said, "Young man, you ain't Moses." Daddy said, "Furthermore, you are going to read your poem in church, and you are going to read it well. Do you understand?"

I am very careful even now about what I ask God for. If I face suffering, like when I had heart surgery, I ask God to help me not to be a wimp about it.

I never got that double-barreled, twenty-gauge shotgun, but I think Daddy had more to do with that than God.

I was told that the reading went well. Unfortunately, I threw that poem away.

A sidebar on Calvin:

Howard Allred, a Duke Divinity student, was assigned to Hickory Grove Methodist Church in about 1950. He was a most dynamic man. He built our membership up and brought in members who had never been to church. During one summer revival, he persuaded Calvin to attend our revival. Calvin came in a brand-new pair of Red Camel, low-back overalls. Those of you who grew up wearing overalls understand that the low-back models

were some farmers' formal wear. Calvin had on a starched white shirt with the sleeves turned up two cuff lengths. His hair was newly cut and oiled down. He had on new wing-tipped shoes. No one had ever seen Calvin so done up. The preacher's sermon the night was on the evils of alcohol. During the sermon, to make a point, the preacher raised his arms and shouted, "I don't know how much a pint of whiskey costs." In a high-pitched, raspy voice, Calvin shouted out, "About $2.50 a pint." Things were quiet momentarily, but soon the congregants erupted in laughter. Calvin turned red and seemed confused.

As far as I know, Calvin never attended church again.

# The Power of Humility

In the fall of 1962 Pomona Pipe Products of Greensboro, North Carolina, transferred me to the crossroads
village of Gulf, North Carolina, to supervise construction
of a new sanitary clay sewer pipe plant. We built a new
plant alongside an existing plant. I was twenty-six years
old at the time and had never supervised workers before.
I was inexperienced but extremely proud of my new job.
Thinking back, I was probably the only one willing to
relocate to this somewhat remote area.

The job required me to assemble a crew of about thirty
skilled, semiskilled, and unskilled laborers. The task was
not supposed to be difficult, as there was a large pool of
all categories available in the area. I put the word out that
I was hiring, but almost no one showed up to apply. I
should mention that this was back when women were not
considered for jobs as welders, pipe fitters, carpenters, or
construction laborers; we were looking for men only.

One of the first men I interviewed was Hugh Clark,
a pitiful-looking soul who walked into the construction
office on a cold day. He was wearing too-large, well-worn
army surplus clothes. Several of his teeth were missing,

and the remaining teeth were partially rotted. His socks were visible through the toes of his shoes. He was so shy that he hardly spoke.

Finally he said, barely audibly, "Mr. Gus over at the store said you might give me a job, but if you don't have one, it's okay." Mr. Gus Murchison owned a local country store and had been extremely helpful introducing me around the area. I felt like he would not have mentioned me to Hugh Clark if Hugh were not a good man.

I asked Hugh a few questions.

"Do you have a job now?"

"Yessuh, I work at the brickyard."

"What do you do there?"

"I do whatever they tell me to."

"What hours do you work?"

"I work forty hours every other week."

"How much money do you earn?"

"Do what?"

"What do they pay you?"

"Dollar twenty-five," he said.

"Do you have a family?"

"Yessuh, four children."

That last answer did it. I knew I was going to hire him. He didn't say "young'uns" or "kids." For the first time in our conversation he smiled, and he had a look of immense pride and pure love as he said, "Four children." It was no wonder about his looks. To raise a family on his income in a day when there were no forms of entitlement or safety nets had to be a struggle.

I hired Hugh at $1.35 an hour, which was ten cents per hour above the minimum wage at the time. I promised him forty hours per week with time-and-a-half for all hours over forty. When I told him he would also have health insurance for himself and his family, he said, "Mr. Thornton, you don't have to do all that."

I eventually assigned Hugh to assist a highly skilled welder. The welder had a terrible expression on his face when I introduced Hugh as his helper. When my boss came down from Greensboro for the first time after I hired Hugh, he actually scolded me.

"What in the name of God are you going to do with that little man?"

I told my boss the story of why I hired Hugh and admitted that his story touched me. "Besides, I may need a man who will do anything I tell him to."

My boss went on about how you can't let emotions enter into a business decision—a comment that has been disproved over and over in my long management career. One may not always yield to emotion, but emotion should be considered in all of life's decisions.

But those who already knew Hugh kept encouraging me, saying, "You won't be sorry. Hugh is a really good man."

From his first day on the job, I knew we had a winner in Hugh. He stood willing to do any work he was assigned. He had to be told to take a break. He took his work so seriously that, on one occasion, when he was using both hands to assist a welder, he had drainage from his nose hanging to his waist. Rather than interrupt his work, he let it hang there. I have never before or since met a man so appreciative of his job.

I hired Hugh on his week off at the local brick company. On the following Monday, the manager of our existing plant called me into his office and introduced me to one of the owners of the plant where Hugh had been working. I was given a very cold reception. I was told in no uncertain terms that the local plants had an arrangement that they would not hire each others' laborers, and if I were going to fit in, I damn well better play by the rules.

I was young and full of piss and vinegar, so I allowed as how I would not join a conspiracy against the workers in the area. The plant manager, unforgettable himself in the mean-to-people category, warned me that when I completed the plant construction, I would be working for him and I better not forget it. I made it clear that Hugh was staying and that was that, and furthermore, I would never work for anyone who would participate in a conspiracy that prevented employees from their right to move about in pursuit of a better life.

I realized after that event why Hugh was so shy about asking for a job. After I hired Hugh, the dam burst on applicants. I learned that the local labor force was aware of the conspiracy and they were afraid to seek employment elsewhere unless they were out of work, for fear of losing their jobs.

Reflecting on the situation, I realized that it took a lot of courage for Hugh to ask for that job. He did ask and, in his humble way, was responsible for breaking up a management conspiracy against laborers in Chatham and Lee Counties, much as Rosa Parks had broken down a racial barrier seven years earlier. On December 1, 1955, in Montgomery Alabama, Rosa Parks made history by refusing to obey bus driver James Blake's order that she give up her seat to make room for a white passenger. Hugh Clark didn't go down in history, but he made a difference in a few lives.

Hugh helped build the new clay-grinding plant. Since the new plant was to mate with the existing plant, we needed to have a benchmark elevation reading. One of the existing grinding plant columns was to be used to obtain this reading. All the columns in the existing grinding plant were covered quite deeply in clay. I pointed to a column and told Hugh to dig out that footing and, when he finished, to go back and continue sorting out the metal that he had been working on. No one was around the area, so I left him alone. I went to a meeting with our general contractor that lasted a very long time. Then I took lunch and eventually went back to check the footing that Hugh had uncovered.

When I approached the site I saw a shovel point pitching clay out of a hole. Hugh had actually dug all the way to the bottom and all the way around the column footing and had nearly dug the entire footing out from under the column. Well, after all, I did say, "Hugh, dig that column footing out." I did not have the heart to correct him, so I said, "Great job, Hugh," and had someone else fill the hole back in the next day after getting the benchmark elevation reading. I pretended that all that digging was necessary.

One day, the welder Hugh was working with asked him to hold two long, thin pieces of metal while the welder tacked them together. The chore only required that the metal be held momentarily. Hugh was to hold the pieces at a right angle to each other. Bill the welder said he heard Hugh saying, "Umm oh, umm oh, umm oh." Bill stopped and looked around. Hugh was still holding the metal and it was red hot, about six inches from his hands. Hugh was not about to turn loose without instructions to do so.

The construction project required that a lot of equipment components be hoisted up to different heights for assembly. I bought a thousand feet of three-quarter-inch hemp rope and five sets of block-and-tackle assemblies. From this material, we built five sets of block-and-tackle hoists. We kept these hoists stored in a small building on a flat area at the top of a bank about twenty feet high.

One day I said, "Hugh, go up to the storage building and bring us a block-and-tackle hoist." The way up to the building was either to climb up that high bank or to take a longer path around a building. Hugh took off up the bank, which on this particular day was sloppy wet and very muddy. I remember thinking that Hugh, in his excitement to do a quick job of it, was taking a shortcut.

In a few minutes we heard a commotion. We looked in the direction of the shuffling noise and saw Hugh sliding down that muddy bank, completely covered with ropes and hoist paraphernalia. Several of us ran over to assist him. When he finished tumbling to the bottom of the bank, we untangled him from the ropes, blocks, and wooden pulley wheels. While he was lying on the ground, he looked up to me and, with a hangdog expression, said, "Mr. Thornton, I didn't know which one you wanted so I brought 'em all." That was pure Hugh.

Funny thing about Hugh's mishaps: no one ever laughed at him. He was one of the most loved men we ever had working on that project. After the plant was finished, I did stay on as plant engineer, and of course I kept Hugh with me.

Oh, the plant manager who had been part of the conspiracy? He was terminated before we finished the new plant.

If Hugh Clark were not already etched indelibly in my heart and memory, his father's funeral clinched the deal.

In the early 1970s, Hugh's father died. By then I was

plant manager. I made it a practice to attend the funerals of employees and their immediate families, so I attended Hugh's father's funeral. His service was conducted at Antioch Christian Church, an old, picturesque, white clapboard-sided building a few miles from the small village of Goldston, North Carolina. I arrived at the church late, which was highly unusual for me as I am habitually on time.

When I arrived, the unpaved, unmarked yard was filled with cars. I surveyed the area looking for a parking place. I saw a long gap in a row of cars parked parallel along a dirt and graveled drive. *This is great*, I thought. It was wide enough for me to drive straight in without having to back in. So I drove front-first into a ditch about five feet deep.

Luckily, I could open the door, get out of the car, and climb out of the ditch. I took a quick look at my car and, walking away, thought, *Looks like no damage. Not to worry, there are plenty of people at the funeral who will help me get my car out of the ditch after the service.* I glanced back at my car as I rushed away. I could see the drain plug on my transmission. My car was belly hung on the bank of that ditch.

This was my first visit to Antioch. Everyone was inside by then. The church had gone through several renovations—a wing here, a wing there. It was impossible to distinguish where the front door was. I took a chance and dashed in what I thought to be the entrance. I quietly took a seat in what seemed to be a small seating area. The service was already in progress. The minister announced that the choir would sing "How Great Thou Art." Folks in my section stood to sing. I was in the bloody choir! I sat there red-faced throughout the service. I had to sit there under the stare of the biggest gossip who worked in our plant. I thought I would never live that incident down.

These things are enough to qualify Hugh Clark as unforgettable, but what I learned from this humble, simple man is what put him with others at the top of my "most unforgettable people" list. These lessons have helped shape my philosophy:

I learned from Hugh that everyone needs recognition and, if given deserved praise, they will become the best they can be.

I learned that no one should be overlooked as a source of inspiration.

I learned that if we aren't careful, we wind up exploiting the weak among us.

Hugh Clark became a part of my life in 1962 and remains a part of what I have become to this day.

When I was fired from Pomona Pipe Products—an event that launched my real career—I looked for Hugh on the job and told him how much knowing him had meant to my life.

Uncharacteristically, he stopped working, shook my hand, and said with moist eyes, "Mr. Thornton, you sho' are good to po' people."

Yes, Hugh, I understand. I've been "po' people."

# That Was Simple

In the early 1960s I owned a 1958 Triumph TR3 sports car. I was told when I bought the car that the engine tended to skip badly at a road speed of about fifty miles per hour. This didn't sound like a problem to me as I planned to use the car only around Greensboro, North Carolina. The route to and from work was through town, and I really wanted that car. Besides, I would probably never go more than fifty-five miles per hour anyway. I learned that wanting something really badly can bring on complicated problems.

Shortly after I bought that TR3, my job required me to travel to our plant in Gulf, North Carolina, some fifty miles east of Greensboro. Being limited to fifty miles per hour became a nuisance, so I took the car into the local Triumph dealership for a fix. After attempts by several mechanics, no fix could be found. I took the blasted thing to several shops, but to no avail.

On one of my trips to the Gulf plant, Max Smith, a mechanic in the Gulf plant office, was admiring my cute little sports car. I told him that it was losing its cuteness.

I explained to Max the problem I was having. I told him about the many mechanics who had attempted to fix the problem, and Max asked if he could take a look.

Max had quit school in eighth grade and had no additional training. He loved to tell people about his education, or lack thereof. I think that, in a way, he was bragging to emphasize his reputation of being able to fix anything.

I was thinking that Max probably just wanted to drive my TR3. I told him he was welcome to try, but that I was leaving in an hour. With that, Max sped off in my car.

When it came time for me to head back to Greensboro, I walked in to see Max wearing a huge smile. He said proudly, "I got 'er fixed. Let's take 'er for a spin."

We took off down Route 421. When we got to a long, straight stretch, Max, in his words, "showered down on it." In no time we were going eighty miles per hour, with no cutting back.

I asked Max, "What in the world did you do, and how did you do it so quickly?"

He said, "After all 'em smart mechanics done worked on it, I said to myself, *It got to be sump'n simple. Ain't no use in doing the same things they been doing.* So I start back at the gas tank and followed the line 'til I fount a little petcock. I checked on it and fount hit had been clogging up, so I jes clent it out."

That was simple!

I was relating this story to the plant manager, Jim Wade, at Lynchburg Foundry in Lynchburg, Virginia. Lynchburg Foundry makes cast-iron water pipe, and Jim told me a story about their metallurgy going off a year or two ago. They discovered the problem through a special test after noticing the product quality was deteriorating. After checking product from previous years, it became clear that the problem had been progressing slowly. It was the kind of problem that took a long time to show up in the field.

The company called in top metallurgists from the best universities, but no one could identify the problem. With the product quality steadily in decline, Jim said to himself, just as Max had said to me, *It has got to be something simple that we're just overlooking*. So he started at the first step in the process, where the scrap iron used in making the pipe was unloaded. The next step was putting a measured tonnage into the cupola. In the cupola-charging procedure, two scoop-type shovels of a mineral were cast into the scrap iron before melting it. Jim asked the employee responsible for this step in the process how long he had been with Lynchburg Foundry.

The employee replied, "Twelve years."

Seeing that the scoop shovel was well worn, Jim asked, "How long have you had that shovel?"

"It's the one they gave me when I came to work here." There was the answer: The shovel was worn to half of its original length.

That was simple!

You don't have to be a genius to solve life's problems. Just always look for a simple solution first.

I have never had formal training in counseling, but through the years, employees have come to me with a

myriad of personal problems. Based on my experience I have concluded that a huge share of problems is rooted in mismanagement of money.

A woman who once worked for me got into deeper and deeper financial trouble. She raised horses, which is a very expensive hobby. Having worked around me for several years, she must have learned that I could manage money, so she asked me to help her with her budget. I told her to bring in every credit card statement, every check written, and a list of every dollar spent within the last year. It was immediately clear, after looking at a few months' expenses, that she was spending more than half of her take-home pay on her horses.

When I showed her the numbers, I said, "You can't solve your money problems unless you give up your horses."

She replied, "That is not going to happen."

I suggested that she start by giving up one at a time until she got her budget under control.

She said again, "That is not going to happen."

I gave her papers back to her and said, "Well, I suppose we're through." We parted ways eventually. She ruined her credit and lost her home to foreclosure.

That problem could have been simple to avoid.

Simple concepts—like "Don't spend more than you earn"—could solve many problems, if followed. Through my years of informal counseling, I have found violation of this particular concept to be the number-one cause of people's problems. Health issues brought on by stress and even divorce often originate in mismanagement of money.

Now, that concept is so simple, I wonder why our government doesn't follow it!

# Profane Words, Generous Acts

One of my first jobs in management at Pomona Pipe Products, after we finished constructing the plant, was as plant engineer. In this position I was responsible for all general engineering duties, including machine design and installation, as well as plant maintenance. Both these functions required a lot of parts and supplies, so salesmen were always calling us. Some of those salesmen were real characters. They provided a kind of continuing education for me, in a technical sense, and left me with a genuine appreciation for salespeople. Some of these relationships went on for a number of years, and their regular sales calls became visits that were part professional and part social. I didn't realize at the time that someday I, myself, would become a salesman. Had I known it, I would have tried to learn more from Harry Sigley.

Harry was about six-feet-two—a barrel-chested man who stood military erect. He had thick white hair that he kept in a crew cut. It was not just any crew cut. His cut was so perfectly cared for, it looked as if it came from a box. The hairs were about one and one-half inches long

and left his head pointing up and out at about a forty-
five-degree angle, as if to say, "Onward and upward!"
Harry was firm and muscled and looked as if he was a
regular at a gym. He always wore a short-sleeved white
shirt and a necktie. His shirts were about one size smaller
than needed for a proper fit, so that any movement of his
arms would reveal flexed muscles.

The only characteristic Harry had that belied his manly
appearance was his voice. Whenever he got excited while
telling a story, which was often, his voice would rise higher
and higher, and his eyes would grow larger and larger.

Harry was one of those salesmen who sold mundane
mill supplies. Like so many other salesmen, he carried a
huge mill supply catalog that must have contained thou-
sands of items. He maintained customer loyalty through
his unique personality and storytelling skills. He could
tell you what he ate for breakfast in a way that would
entertain you as well as any stand-up comedian. Long
after I had moved up in the organization and no longer
dealt directly with salesmen, I would often go back to the
supply room to see Harry on his regular monthly visit.

All visitors to our company parked in sight of my
office. One day I saw Harry drive up, but he took a long
time getting out of his car. When he finally did, I could
tell something was wrong. Although he got out on the
opposite side of the car from my view, as he came around
to full view I could see that he was on crutches. His left leg
was bandaged up above his knee, causing his leg to stick
out in a stiff pose. His walk was awkward and slow. I went

out and offered to assist him to the supply room, which also was Harold Trogdon's office—the buyer. Harry was almost in tears. I took the catalogs he was struggling with and asked, "Harry, what in the world happened to you?"

"Wait 'til I can sit down, and I'll tell you."

Harold and I got Harry comfortably seated, and he told us his story.

"I took a few days vacation last week. My wife didn't want to go nowheres so I thought I would paint my boat trailer. I was sanding off the rust spots, and at one point I put my left foot on that angle iron along the trailer frame and was going to stand up on it. My G–d–n foot slipped, and I scraped all the meat off my shin bone almost up to my kneecap. It happened last Tuesday. It got infected, so I went to the doctor on Friday."

The pitch of his voice grew higher as his eyes got larger and larger.

"Boy, this thing has been painful. My first day back at work was yesterday. I had to call on the utility director over at NC State, who is on the third floor. I get on the elevator, and push the button for the third floor. When we reach the third floor, the door opens and naturally my left leg sticks out the elevator door first. Here comes a blind man whupping the wall with his cane looking for the elevator door. He slaps the hell out of my bad leg with that G–d–n white cane. I thought I was going to die! If that ol' son-of-a-bitch wasn't blind, and I was not about to die from the pain, I would have taken that white cane away from him and beat him to death."

Another time I saw Harry get out of his car with his catalogs. He was not walking military erect, so I thought to myself, *Did Harry grow old without me noticing?* I followed him to Harold's office. I was a bit shy about asking if something was wrong with him, but it turned out I didn't have to ask.

After the salutations were over, Harry looked at us one at a time and asked, "Have y'all ever had your prostate massaged?" Without waiting for an answer, he went on. "I stayed in the Siler City Motel last night and never slept a wink. I was so sick." I might explain here that Harry always stayed at the Siler City Motel on the second Tuesday every month. His life was a totally planned routine. He said, "This morning I asked the woman who owns the motel if she knew a doctor that might see me right away. I know her well, and we have become pretty good friends through the years, so she got on the phone and got me an appointment with Dr. Dougan. Do you guys know Dr. Dougan?"

Again, without waiting for an answer, he continued, "I got there on time. A nurse took me to a room and went through the usual nurse things like urine sample, blood pressure, temperature, etc. She then said, 'Undress down to your underwear; the doctor will be in right away.'

"'Thank you, ma'am. I don't mind setting, sick, in a thirty-seven-degree room waiting for a G–d–n doctor.'

"Dr. Dougan eventually came in and asked a few questions. He said, 'Harry, I think you have prostatitis; drop your drawers and bend over that table.'

"He pointed to a table that would take six damn football players to move. I noticed that while he was instructing me, he was putting on a rubber glove. His index finger was shaped like a baseball bat and 'bout half as big. He greez the tip of his finger as I bent over that table. He started with his finger and rammed his fist up my ass to his elbow, whereupon a hand grenade went off. I shoved his table against the wall so hard that it cracked the plaster from floor to ceiling. When I got to where I could finally stand alone, Dr. Dougan said, 'Harry, you do have prostatitis, and I'm going to give you medicine to

clear it up.' Then he said, 'Harry, would you please move my table back to the middle of the room?'

"I said, 'I don't believe I can budge it, but if you'll ram your fist up my ass again, I'll take it upstairs for you.'"

I don't know how many of Harry's stories were factually true, but we died laughing. It takes a different kind of sense of humor to turn pain into laughter. I believe that Harry taught me to find humor in any of life's situations.

I don't recall Harry ever asking us to buy something or trying to impress us with his sales ability. I think we bought from him so he would keep coming to see us the second Tuesday of every month.

Harry was one of the most giving people I have ever known. He could tell many stories of people he had helped in numerous ways, often accompanied by tears.

I became a salesman myself when my business partners and I started an engineering and construction company. I had demanded the sales job because it appeared to involve a lot of fun and very little hard work, but selling turned out to be harder than I had expected. Except for the cursing, I used Harry's style in my own sales efforts. A customer who wants to see you visit will more than likely buy from you. I am generally uncomfortable with the profane use of God's name, but Harry's cursing didn't seem to bother me. He was a good man, and the way I look at it, in the end a person's words are more important for the intent than for the content.

# Natural Leader

Our Sunday school class recently held lessons on the life of Moses and his being asked by God to lead the Israelites out of Egypt and out of slavery. Moses was a reluctant leader, making excuses time after time for why it should not be him who should take on the task. He offered all the excuses he could come up with. God answered them all, so he finally accepted the challenge. The study of Moses offers many valuable lessons in leadership that I have used in my own management career, including how to build an organization. Moses was exhausting himself by micromanaging the movement of the Israelites out of bondage. Moses's father-in-law, Jethro, warned Moses that he could not continue his demanding management style and so offered some valuable advice. He advised Moses to put "ten men over ten" to build a pyramid organization chart, having no more than ten men reporting to any manager, thus allowing a sharing of the day-to-day burdens. This is, as far as I have learned, the first record of what became the modern-day business organization chart. Not much information is available about how Moses chose the leaders, but a careful study of the scriptures gives clues. I bet the same principles are in use today.

Another personal lesson I learned from my study of Moses was how to excel in making excuses, a principle that I have used all too often. But that's another story.

People who have supervised others in an organization and faced the opportunity to choose a leader at some time in their management careers consider it to be one of the most important decisions they ever face. The effect is profound for the organization and even more profound for the life of the person chosen.

At one point in my career I faced the opportunity to fill a supervisory position in a plant that I managed. As usual, my first preference in this situation was to look among the current employees and find someone who had in some way demonstrated natural leadership characteristics. In addition to this primary reason for consideration, I also looked at other factors such as a person's character, sobriety, and attitude. Education was considered only if the position demanded special training, like accounting or engineering.

In this particular case I had observed through time that Charles Saunders had certain leadership qualities.

In a process-type operation, where a production interruption is very costly and harmful, it is imperative to correct that interruption as quickly and completely as possible. Our product was vitrified clay sewer pipe used in city sewer systems. It was fired in tunnel kilns, which qualified it as a process-type industry. If some pipes fell

into the kiln, this was called a kiln wreck, which could lead to one gigantic glass mass requiring a lot of money and many days of lost production. Kiln wrecks were a major failure that got the entire organization involved, but the work to clean up and get back in business was done by the department in which Charles worked. Once before, when we had a kiln wreck, I had observed that the employees looked to Charles for direction, and Charles had taken control although that was not his normal responsibility. All the while, he had directed the cleanup and start-back with friendliness and efficiency. I had filed this information in the back of my mind and determined to watch Charles for consideration for a promotion.

A time came when I needed a supervisor to fill a spot left by a man who went for another position in a local plant, so one day I told Charles I wanted to see him in my office. He arrived in my office at the appointed time with a quizzical expression and nervously sat down. I came right out with it.

"Charles, I want to promote you to supervisor of your department."

Charles looked stunned and started to make Moses-like excuses: "Can't you find someone else? I have never supervised before. I have never done anything but labor." Finally he said, "I only went through the eighth grade."

I explained to Charles that I had thought through all those things thoroughly. He wasn't convinced, so I told him to talk it over with Edna and meet with me in my office the next day.

Charles was surprised that I named his wife. I think bringing Edna into the discussion gave him the impression that I really had given it a lot of thought.

I said, "Oh, and one more thing, Charles. Here is a reading assignment for you. I don't know if you read the Bible or not, but that is not the point, and I am not preaching to you. I think you will read in this assignment a story that parallels what we are discussing." With that, I gave Charles a paper that I had kept in my desk drawer through the years titled "The Fine Art of Making

Excuses." It was about the many excuses Moses gave God when God asked Moses to lead the Israelites out of bondage: *I'm not qualified. I don't have enough education. I don't think it will work. It's not my gift. I don't want to do it.* And finally, *Send someone else.*

When Charles came into my office the next morning, he was relaxed and smiling. He started the conversation by saying, "Edna and I read the article and even read the scriptures that it came from. I have two questions: Do you have the confidence in me that God had in Moses? And will you watch my back like God watched Moses's back?" I answered both questions with a very firm "Yes" and "Yes."

Charles took that job. Within three months he had delivered a measurable improvement in every point used in evaluating manufacturing. My confidence in Charles was confirmed worthy by his performance, and I did have his back on several occasions. Later on, when I needed a supervisor for the shipping department—a position requiring more responsibility and stronger management—I promoted Charles. The success that Charles achieved in his first management position made him a most confident and solid manager. Eventually he was promoted to supervise the entire shipping and delivery department, including managing our trucking company. This job involved responsibility for operations in North Carolina as well as for a company that we owned in Pottstown, Pennsylvania.

All things considered, my and Charles's business relationship was among the best business experiences I have had throughout my long management career. I am very proud that I took the time and effort to encourage him that day in my office. After Charles left Pomona Pipe Products, he successfully owned and operated a popular restaurant in Lee County, North Carolina. A few years ago, Charles died with dignity after suffering with cancer for several years.

Charles Saunders provided me with some wonderful memories that I will forever cherish. *God rest your soul, Charles!*

# A True Love Story

Grace Pew was my secretary when I was working in Raleigh, North Carolina, as an engineering consultant in 1979. Grace grew up in and lived in a farming community near Wilson, North Carolina, in Johnston County. A petite, genteel woman, Grace was the epitome of her namesake, and in spite of being born and brought up poor, she possessed a quiet dignity and could fit in with proper society as if she was a high-bred southern lady.

Grace and I were the same age, and once she learned of my farm family upbringing, she loosened up and shared her own stories about growing up. I have found that Johnston County people are generally hardworking farm folks who take life in an unassuming manner.

Grace asked me once, "Do you think that good marriages are a result of two people dating, falling in love, having a period of courtship, and then saying vows?" My answer was, "No," and before I could elaborate by discussing arranged marriages, mail-order brides, and girls who were traded in marriage to an old man for two goats, Grace said, "I agree," and proceeded to tell me this story.

Grace's mother, Mildred, was the oldest of four girls. Mildred's father died at thirty-five of a heart attack at the height of the Great Depression, leaving her mother, Marcie, with four girls from two to eight years of age. Marcie had very few possessions and no way to make a living. There was a quiet bachelor named Milton living nearby. He had a small farm and tools for raising tobacco. Milton stayed to himself but was considered to be a really good man. He was always the first to show up at the side of a neighbor in need. People wondered why he had never married.

One Sunday afternoon after feeding her four kids Sunday dinner and before the kids had taken off their going-to-church clothes, Marcie announced to them, "Clean up real good, 'cause we are going visiting." After inspecting each child thoroughly, she asked the oldest to help her hook their mule, Molly, to the wagon.

Then Marcie made herself up to look her prettiest, and they headed for bachelor Milton's place on that one-mule wagon.

When they arrived, Milton was standing on the front porch staring at them as they took the long, slow ride up to his house. Marcie wasted no time. She marched right up to Milton and without hesitation said, "Milton, you know that my husband died. Now, I need someone to help me raise these girls. and I think you need a wife. I'm proposing to you. Milton. I will be a good wife to you. I can do all the things that any good farm wife can do, and

do 'em better'n most. Milton, will you marry me and help me raise these children?"

Marcie must have been thinking about it for a while, because she reached in a bag and took out a garment. She handed the garment to Milton and said, "I brung you a shirt, Milton. I sewed it my self."

Grace's Grandmother laughingly says that Milton swallowed hard and said, "I reckon I have room for y'all. I'll pick you up tomorrow."

The next day Milton and Marcie went to see the minister and arranged to get married.

Grace was so interested in her grandmother's story that after she became an adult, she went and interviewed the older people who were neighbors of Milton and Marcie. One woman said that the community was shocked at Marcie's boldness, but as time went by, everyone saw a loving couple with happy children. Milton and Marcie were totally accepted as friends and neighbors, showing true love and devotion to one another by everyone's measure.

The four kids often told stories of being raised by Milton as his very own. They would describe Milton as a really kind, soft-spoken man with a firm hand and wise ways. Grace's mother said that the only time Milton ever came close to anger was when one of the children sassed her mama. He would clear his throat and say, "Be kind to your mama; she put her all into loving you and providing for you young'uns."

Grace's mother remembered reading a book one time and laughing at about the time for supper. Marcie said,

"Girl, get your head out of that book and help me with supper." Milton stepped forward and said, "Let her read. I will help you with supper." That evening as the family was eating supper, Milton looked at Grace's mother and asked, "Can you learn me to read?" She later described that moment as one of the sweetest experiences that she has ever had.

Grace's mother did "learn" Milton to read. In fact, he became an avid reader. Milton seemed to take delight in telling folks down at the country store about something he had read in the paper. He placed a high priority on education and insisted that the girls finish high school, which they did. Finishing high school was rare in that time and place. Most kids quit school to help support the family.

One story that exemplified Milton's kindness and gentle ways was when the family's mule, Molly, got very sick. After examining Molly, the vet told Milton that the poor mule's teeth were infected and would cause her death. He advised Milton that the kind thing to do would be to put Molly down. That night at the supper table, Milton was even quieter than usual. After a while, he said in a choked voice, "I ain't gonna let Molly die. I will never forget that Sunday when I saw her coming down the road pulling that carry-all—the day she brung y'all to me." With that said, Milton went to the old pie safe and took out a jar of white whiskey, which many people back then kept on hand for medicinal purposes. (I still think peppermint candy dissolved in white liquor makes a great cough suppressant.) Milton went to the barn with

a long-necked bottle filled with that whiskey and poured it down Molly's throat. Molly was as good as out in a few minutes. Milton pulled Molly's teeth out with tongs and treated her mouth with disinfectant.

Milton slept in the barn with Molly until she was up and about. From that day on, Milton ground a mixture of grain and hay softened in milk for Molly to eat. He hand-fed her that way until she died a few years later. Milton kept Molly several years beyond her usefulness. It was common practice back then to put down a farm animal that had lost its usefulness and had become a burden on the family.

One elderly neighbor told Grace that no one ever knew Milton's age, but they assumed him to be several years older than Marcie. Milton died before Marcie, and she would often say that life was sure hard to live without him.

Now that is a true love story.

# From One Humanitarian Act,
# a Broader Worldview

As a young man I went to New York City regularly to work toward a master's degree in business administration under the auspices of the American Management Association (AMA). The school was located at 1601 Broadway, and I always stayed at the nearby New York Hilton Hotel at 1335 Avenue of the Americas. Being a country boy I was usually up and about and had eaten breakfast well before class time, so I often wandered the streets of the city before my classes began.

On one cold morning I was walking along Forty-Second Street and observed a commotion about a half-block ahead of me. As I got closer, I saw people stepping off the curb to walk around a feeble-looking elderly lady lying on the icy sidewalk. My first thought was, *Well, well, a typical New York scene. People here are so accustomed to such things that they rush on by without a bother.* When I got closer, I observed a frail woman about eighty years old, weighing no more than ninety pounds, wearing only a flimsy

nightgown, lying there. She had apparently slipped and fallen on the sheet of ice. I could not pass her by.

As I stooped down to check on her, I was taunted by passersby. As I leaned in, I found myself looking into very frightened eyes. I tried to calm her by speaking softly and assuring her that I wanted to help her. I asked her name.

She relaxed a bit and said in an almost inaudible voice, "Angie."

I then asked Angie, "Where do you live?"

She pointed to a narrow stairwell that rose between the John Barleycorn pub and a small retail storefront. I started to lift her gently, being careful to observe any sign of broken bones. With my assistance, Angie rose comfortably. I took my suit jacket off and draped it around her shoulders. She seemed stronger after getting up, so I offered to help her to her place, which was apparently up those stairs. Angie was unsteady as, with my help, she climbed the stairs. At the top of the stairs there was a small landing with a door on the left and a door on the right. The door on the right was open, and Angie stepped toward it. Inside was, as I have since learned, a typical New York City one-room efficiency apartment. There was a Murphy bed lowered into the sleeping position. The apartment was a mess. Leftover food, unwashed dishes, and clothes were scattered about.

I asked Angie if she lived alone.

"Yes," she replied.

"Do you have family nearby?"

"I have a son on Long Island, I think."

"Do you have his number?"

With this question, Angie rambled around the small, cluttered phone desk. I noticed her confusion, so I looked for and found a recipe card with a few phone numbers on it.

"Do you have a son named Greg?" I asked.

She looked a bit bewildered, so I thought, *I will just start with him.* His name was listed twice, and one number had "work" written in parentheses by it. I dialed the number and a man answered. I asked, "Do you have a relative named Angie who lives on forty-Second Street in the city?"

"Yes, I do. What's wrong?" I suppose my southern accent caused him concern.

When I told him that Angie had fallen on the street and that I had brought her up to her apartment, he went ballistic. "What the hell are you doing in my mother's apartment?"

By then I was a bit worldly and could stand toe-to-toe with the likes of him. I shouted, "If you were any kind of a son, I would not have to be helping your mother, and it appears to me that I care more for her right now than you do! She couldn't even remember or call your name! I picked your name out of a lineup on a card by her phone."

He said he was at work and would come by her place when he got off. *What a cold response*, I thought. I left Angie, feeling a bit uncomfortable about her well-being.

The whole day, during my studies, I could not stop thinking of Angie. I decided to go by her place when my classes ended, despite the treatment I had received from her rude son. When I got to her apartment, I knocked and got no response. I waited and knocked again, but still no one answered, so I decided there was nothing more I could do. For some reason, I had failed to make a note of either Angie's phone number or her son's. As there seemed to be no options, I turned and started down the stairs.

I neared the bottom of the stairs, and I saw a well-dressed, middle-aged man starting up the stairs. The man looked up and saw me. The stairwell was quite narrow, so he stepped back onto the street.

I asked him if he was Angie's son.

He told me that he wasn't and asked me, "Who is Angie?"

I told him that Angie lived in an apartment at the top of the stairs. Typical of us southerners, I told him the entire story about what had happened that morning.

He looked a bit humbled and asked me if I was from the South, and I told him I was from North Carolina.

He said, "Leave it to someone from the South to demonstrate humanity to New Yorkers."

We seemed to have some kind of instant bond. He introduced himself as Ken Bretton and asked my name. Ken invited me to have a drink in the John Barleycorn pub. Once we sat down he told me his story.

Ken rented the apartment next door to Angie, but had never seen her. He looked to be a successful man, so I wondered about him living in such a small place. He told me that he was from Indiana and had worked in advertising in New York for twenty years—long enough to have lost some of his rural roots and midwestern humanity, he said. My story made him realize how easy it is to lose one's moral compass in a big city.

As the conversation continued, he explained that he lived with his wife and family in Essex, Connecticut. He maintained the small apartment to use on those bad-weather days and on days when he had late-evening meetings or extremely early-morning ones. His train ride to and from the city could often take up to two hours. Ken asked my reason for being in New York. When I explained why I was in the city, he told me that his advertising firm, McCann Erickson, used AMA for training purposes also.

At about 6 p.m., Ken looked at his watch and said he was meeting some other advertising people at Luchow's, a popular German restaurant, and asked if I had plans for the evening. I replied that I did not, and he told me he would be delighted to have me come along. I was hesitant, but I had learned what a great experience it is to be exposed to various cultures, so I accepted. As we walked to Luchow's, the conversation was like that of old friends. Ken said he was going to tell my story and asked me not to be surprised if I got kidded about being naïve.

The gathering went well, and I was kidded a lot. One jovial dude told me that it is popular for criminals to use an old lady to lure unsuspecting people up to a place to be robbed. Criminals especially like southern folks. I joined right in and was well received. Later, the conversation took a more serious turn. Most of the dozen or so men and women there, representing a variety of races and cultures, lamented the loss of human interest and concern for other people. At least three people brought up the Good Samaritan story from the Bible.

I never dreamed how the events of that day would lead to such a rich expansion of my world.

When Ken and I started to go our separate ways, he asked if I had plans to be back in New York. I explained that I would be back for several one- or two-week periods within the next year. He said, "Call me when you get your schedule, and I will meet you and give you a key to my little apartment. You can use my apartment anytime you come up." I asked Ken to call me if he ever got any word on Angie. Ken called in about a week and told me that someone was moving into Angie's apartment, but they knew nothing about Angie's situation. We never heard a word about her or what had what happened to her. I only hope that the falling episode led to her being moved to a place where she could receive loving care.

About three months later I was scheduled for a two-week class at AMA. I called Ken, and he met me with a key and invited me to visit him and his family in Essex for the weekend. He had a lovely family, and we had a good visit. If anyone wants to get a sense of how pretty the New England coast is, Essex Village, Connecticut, would be a good destination. I rode the train to and from Essex. *The Yankees can have that rat race*, I thought.

On my next week in New York City, Ken invited me to the home of a person who was hosting a book signing for Jerry Della Femina. The host's apartment covered the entire top floor of a high-rise apartment building. It was like something you see in movies. The people there were an enjoyable mix of musicians, artist, authors, and civic leaders, both gay and straight. It was the most diverse group I have ever been with.

Jerry Della Femina was a character among characters. I was told beforehand that, as a young man, he had built from scratch one of the most successful advertising firms in the world.

Jerry was supposedly a genius-level student in an Ivy League school. He was sought out and hired by a large advertising firm in New York City. The firm expected big things from Jerry, so upon his arrival to the firm, they had him sit in on creative sessions, hoping to speed up his learning curve. The firm was invited to bid on a campaign to introduce the Panasonic company and its products to the U.S. market. Two other large advertising firms were competing for the contract, and it was a winner-take-all situation. Of course, the loser would forfeit all of the money that they had invested in the campaign. What they were to present, if accepted by Panasonic, would be exactly what potential customers for Panasonic products would see or hear on TV, radio, billboards, and such.

The campaign that Jerry's employer was going to present was fully prepared except for a slogan or jingle that they hoped would become iconic for Panasonic, as recognizable as the Pillsbury doughboy or Ronald McDonald.

Late one evening just before their deadline, the top executives were in a desperate attempt to come up with a slogan or jingle with the impact like the above or something along the caliber of the cigarette commercial, "Winston tastes good like a cigarette should."

Jerry was to listen and learn, but suddenly he spoke up, "I got it, I got it!" With all eyes on him, Jerry shouted out, "What about 'From those same wonderful folks who brought you Pearl Harbor'?"

Jerry was promptly fired, but he had the title for his book and the freedom to start his own firm. That ain't bad for one attempt at humor in a tense moment.

Somewhere here in our home I have a signed copy of Jerry's book that he gave me as a gift. Jerry and I told jokes and laughed a lot. He told me that everything I said was funny, even if it was just because of the way I said it.

The last time I went to New York and used Ken's apartment, I arrived in the afternoon at about 5 p.m. to find a note on the door. The note read, "Hi LaVerne. I am staying over tonight but you're welcome to sleep on the couch. I have a couple meeting me at the apartment at six. We are going to dinner and to a play. I have a ticket for you and would like for you to join us." I had no plans for the evening and decided that it would be another good experience.

Ken arrived about five. His friends were there at six. He introduced them as Bob and Taylor. Bob was short and very fat. Taylor was quite tall. Both were bald, with what little hair left being almost shaven. They were dressed in conservative blue suits. We had a pleasant dinner with most of the conversation being about the advertising business. Most of the discussions were prompted by my many questions about the workings of their world. Ken asked at one point if Bob looked familiar to me. I responded by saying I did not recognize him. Taylor said that Bob was one of the persons standing in line at a McDonald's restaurant in their current TV ad.

The play was titled *A Day in the Park* and had not-so-subtle references to the gay lifestyle. At one point I glanced toward Bob and saw that he was holding Taylor's hand. I had no doubt that Ken was straight as straight could be. I, however, with my background, was a bit shocked, and I tried to show no reaction. The evening ended with handshakes and the usual "Let's do this again sometime." Bob and Taylor hailed a cab, and Ken and I walked back to the apartment. I never commented on what I had observed between the couple. I did, however, begin to mellow in my attitude toward gay people and have grown more accepting of them.

After that, Ken and I would occasionally talk, but time and geography eventually brought our communication to an end.

I have many stories of events that evolved from my brief encounter with Angie and my chance meeting with Ken. These stories of rich and diverse experiences changed my life in some ways. I learned to embrace life fearlessly, enthusiastically, and without prejudice. I learned that overcautiousness shields a person from many exciting opportunities.

Accepting the involvement with the variety of people that Ken introduced to me was a nonissue. My parents taught us to be receptive to all people. Lucille and I, in turn, exposed our children to as many diverse people and situations as we possibly could.

During a time when all types of organizations were rushing to train their folks in diversity, our family did not require retraining.

What a loss our lives would have suffered if prejudice had kept these people out of our lives!

Thank you, Angie. I can not relive, in memory, some of the momentous times of my life without thinking of you.

# Whatever It Takes

In the mid-1960s I was named assistant plant manager at Pomona Pipe Products in Gulf, North Carolina. One of my responsibilities was human resources, which required that I sign off on all job applicants. In doing so, I met some real characters. Joe was one of those. I knew the first time I saw Joe that there would be some good stories to follow.

One cold day I was returning from my rounds around the plant. My routine, as usual, took me through a side door to the office building. The door opened into a small room used by job seekers to fill out applications for employment. The walls of this room were lined with eight-by-ten photographs of the company president shaking hands with various employees while handing them an "employee longevity plaque" for having been with the company for ten, fifteen, twenty years, or more. One day as I was passing through this room, I noticed a man standing there holding a job application and staring at those photos. He turned to me and asked, "Why is ever-body giving that man a picture?" If that wasn't a laugh-out-loud funny question, his appearance certainly was. I asked his name, in an effort to control my laughter. He said, "My name is Joe."

Joe was of medium height and build. He had on bib-type overalls and a thin, white, short-sleeved T-shirt even though it was a cold winter's day. His shoes were worn out, and he wore no socks. He had on a leather baseball-style cap. The leather bill was so frayed that the cardboard liner that kept the bill stiff and shaped looked like pages of a book that had been wet and had dried all wrinkled and thick. The reason I go into detail here is because Joe did become a part of a lot of stories and seemed to always be dressed in those same clothes. He had one eye that was straight and one that was crooked. He moved his head from side to side, giving the impression that he was checking you out with one eye and then the other. You could never tell which eye he was looking at you with, and when talking with Joe, you would adopt his style of shifting your own head to keep time with him. We hired Joe and placed him on a simple, repetitive job. He did well and seemed happy.

On one of our first warm days in spring, Joe showed up for work barefooted and wearing no shirt. His supervisor tried, to no avail, to explain to Joe why he had to wear a shirt and shoes. I intervened and firmly told Joe that he would have to leave and not to return to work without shoes on and wearing a shirt. Joe did as told but never understood our strange ideas.

Not long after hiring Joe, we changed health insurance companies and got a much-improved policy. The policy required that every employee had to sign up. Joe held out and held out, just refusing to sign up. It became so frustrating that I sent for him to meet with me in my office. When Joe came in, I offered him a seat across from me at my desk. I simply slid the form toward him and said, "Joe, you either sign the insurance application or I going to fire you."

Joe said, "Okay," and signed.

I asked, "Joe, why have you been so stubborn about signing up?"

Joe said, "You never 'splained it to me like 'at a-fore."

One day my secretary Bobbi Jean asked me if I thought Joe had a six-year-old daughter. I replied that I doubted it because of his age. Bobbi Jean said we had received a claim on his insurance account for a hospital stay for a six-year-old girl. We called Joe over to inquire into the claim.

Joe immediately said, "Oh, no, that ain't my girl, it's my neighbor's little girl. She be sick and they ain't got no inshonce, so I let 'em use mine." It was hard to convince Joe that he could not do that. His argument was "I pay for it, so why can't I use it any way I want to?"

The unemployment rate was so low during that time that jobs in our area went unfilled, so companies were reluctant to terminate trouble employees. In fact, we increased our effort to work with our problem employees to retain them. During this time Joe developed a habit of being late for work. Since he was a part of a team, it was especially important that he be at work on time. Our frontline supervisors had just completed training on how to work with problem employees. Joe's supervisor, Charles Saunders, was gung-ho to use his new skills to try and modify Joe's behavior. Charles called Joe into his office at the end of his shift, even telling him he would get overtime pay for staying late. The meeting didn't last long. Charles reported to me after the little session with Joe. He was laughing hysterically. He said that right at the height of his effort to use all his newly acquired skills, Joe looked at him with that one crooked eye and one straight eye and practically screamed, "I done heered all dis shit I'm gonna heer." With that, Joe stomped out. Joe was at work early the next morning and was rarely late after that.

It was general knowledge around the plant that I would help employees with personal problems. One summer day I was passing Joe's workstation, and Joe motioned me over. He said, "You gotta talk to my wife."

"What about, Joe?"

"I got de crabs."

"And you want me to tell your wife that you have crabs?"

"She know I got 'em. Tell her I got 'em here."

There was word around the plant that a contractor working on an addition to our plant had used our toilet facilities and had introduced an ample population of crabs into our plant. I said, "Okay, Joe. Give me your phone number, and I will call her."

"No, she wanna see you."

I started to shake a bit long about then but agreed to talk to his wife in person if she would come to my office. I was hoping upon hope that this would end the whole thing.

"When?" Joe asked.

I suggested that, since his shift ended at three-thirty, he could pick her up and meet me back at the plant at five. "How about day after tomorrow?" I asked.

"How 'bout today? She really pissed."

Anxious to get it over with and seeing as how Joe wasn't going to turn it loose, I agreed. Promptly at five, I saw Joe and wife get out of his rusty old truck. I immediately thought of the Clampetts of the *Beverly Hillbillies*. Joe had on a pair of brand-new Red Camel overalls; a clean, starched, white shirt; and shiny cordovan wing-tipped shoes that he had bought through our company program.

His thick black hair appeared to be larded down. The hair actually added a touch of class to old Joe and reminded me of the *Great Gatsby* era. Mrs. Joe was plainly dressed, no makeup, with her hair in a bun. I welcomed them in and showed them to a chair. For a while none of us spoke. Finally, I asked Mrs. Joe, "So, you want to talk to me?"

"Yeah!"

"Is it about Joe's condition?"

"Yeah." Having heard her speak only one word, albeit twice, I started to wonder about the size of Mrs. Joe's vocabulary. Wanting desperately to get on with it, I said, "We have some nasty people working here on a construction project and they are passing crabs around." As a clincher, I said, "Lots of people have caught them here."

To my surprise—no, actually I was shocked—she blurted out, "How do you know?"

I impulsively blurted back, "Cause I got 'em too." I suppose, under the circumstances, that was an acceptable white lie.

They left, and I washed the blush off my face. The next day I was anxious to go by to see Joe. I was going to explain to him that I didn't really have crabs, but then I said to myself, *Don't stir sleeping crabs.* When I approached Joe, he simply said, "She ain't pissed no mo."

Folks like Joe provide a valuable service in an organization. They keep your wits tuned because they hear a different drummer, or think outside the box, or whatever those clichés are.

# Promises, Promises

A few weeks ago I was rifling through my catch-all drawer—you know, the place where we all throw things that we don't have a use for but don't want to throw away—and ran across a shoe repair ticket that was five years old. Out of curiosity, I took the ticket to the shoe repair shop. The same man was working at his cobbler's bench. I produced the repair ticket and, without blinking, he grinned and said, "They will be ready tomorrow." Actually, the man was kidding, but it started me thinking. At any moment in time, probably 80 percent of humans are waiting for 80 percent of other humans to keep some promise they made. It could be a promise to repair a car by a certain time, arrive at your house to repair plumbing, or any of a multitude of unfulfilled promises.

A friend of mine said he had a car that stayed in the body shop for so long that the depreciation reduced the value of the car to half the repair costs.

We bought a new range and oven three years ago—the slide-in type. We aimed to purchase an almond-colored stove to match all of our other appliances, but the clerk at

Lowe's informed us that almond had been discontinued by all manufacturers and had been replaced with bisque.

"Not to worry," said the clerk, "the bisque will look great alongside the almond." We had our new stove delivered and installed. When we stood back to admire our new purchase, we saw a most hideous combination of colors. Some color genius had developed a color that, when displayed alongside almond, would make a buzzard puke.

For the sake of harmonious living, we replaced all of our appliances. No doubt, this was the aim of the appliance manufacturers when they made their color change.

Well, the touch control panel went bad on the range just before Thanksgiving and was still unrepaired by Christmastime. I might add here that Thanksgiving and Christmas are the only times we use our oven. Being only Lucille and me, we do most oven cooking in a small toaster oven. Other times of the year, I kiddingly say that Lucille stores cookbooks in the regular oven.

Eventually we were told that the model we had was discontinued and would be replaced with a new model because parts were no longer available for the discontinued model. To our huge relief, the new oven was available in bisque.

Added to the promises that are not kept on time is the problem of implied promises. An example is a chiropractor who keeps you coming back for appointment after appointment, leaving you with hope for a cure, while the real reason is to gain job security for the doctor, therapist, and others.

I have always enjoyed the jokes that President Reagan told, and one of his favorite stories was about a couple in the Soviet Union. The Soviet Union at the time could not deliver goods and services to its people. The couple had gone to an auto dealer in 1972 and ordered a car.

The dealer said, "Your car will be delivered June 3, 1985."

The husband asked, "Will that be in the morning or afternoon?"

The salesman asked, "What difference does it make?"

The husband replied, "The plumber is coming in the morning."

Along the same lines, although not actually in the Bible, I can imagine the following situation could have occurred with Abe Methuselah, the dude who lived to be 969 years old. Methuselah was born in 1221 BCE and died in 252 BCE. Methuselah carried a little drawstring purse all his life. It was made from a camel's testicle bag with a drawstring made from sheep gut. Old Meth's belongings were discovered many years later by Rachael, his first cousin thirty-three times removed on his mother's side, his mother being Mary Magdalene the first. When Rachael opened his little leather drawstring purse, she found two small pieces of parchment: a five-hundred-year-old sandal repair ticket from "Camel Saddles Are Us," and a chiropractor's appointment card. When Rachael presented the repair ticket to Omar at "Camel Saddles Are Us," without blinking, the cobbler said with a grin, "They will be ready tomorrow."

Rachael stopped by the office of the chiropractor, Dr

Sol Sawbones, to cancel Methuselah's appointment. Sol expressed his condolences and then said, "It's a shame he died. I could have fixed his lower back pain with just 1,173 more appointments if he had kept drinking five gallons of water a day and avoided any food containing molecules." Rachael gritted her teeth, acknowledged Dr Sol's remarks, and entered a note on her parchment note pad to pick up old Meth's sandals the next day.

Breaking promises is spoken of in the Bible: "If a man vow a vow unto the Lord, or swear an oath to bind his soul with a bond; he shall not break his word, he shall do according to all that proceeded out of his mouth" (Numbers 30:2).

With all this negative stuff, I have to add that I have, on occasions, had my faith in humankind renewed.

Once, in about 1970, I loaned a down-and-out young man nine hundred dollars to purchase products for resale. The products were required to be purchased in order for the young man to become a distributor in a multilevel marketing company. After several years of not being paid, I counted the money lost.

One day in a restaurant, about ten years later, a down-and-out looking man whom I did not recognize walked up to me and asked, "Do you remember me?"

I replied that I did not.

He then pulled out some folded money and said, "It's taken me a long time to save up the nine hundred dollars I owe you, but here it is. I tried to figure the interest, but I ain't good at math. So, if it ain't right, you just tell me how much it is."

I assured him that what he gave me was adequate.

He asked for and received my forgiveness. He thanked me, hugged me, and declared, "I ain't felt this good in a long time."

I gave him back one hundred dollars and said, "If you want to really feel good, give this to someone in need."

A few years later, another unexpected thing occurred.

I stopped by the same man's mobile home sales business and congratulated him on his business success. For some reason, I was not upset that he took so long to pay me back—so long that I had written the money off. Seeing him in a successful business more than paid me back. Character pays off.

An ancient Chinese culture gave such high priority to keeping promises that they used a story to teach their children its importance.

> Xu Shaoyu was from Qiantang. In early August of the third year of Guang Xu, he borrowed one hundred silver coins from Yi Zhai. They did not write a receipt. Instead, they orally agreed that the money would be returned one year later. In August of the next year, Xu Shaoyu was critically ill. In his last moment, he had been talking to himself while lying in bed, "It is almost time for me to return the money. What should I do if I die?"
>
> His wife said, "You are so ill and we have spent so much on medicine. In addition, you don't have a written document about the borrowed money. Therefore, you don't have to worry about returning the money."
>
> Xu Shaoyu said, "He did not write a receipt because he trusted me. How can I not keep my promise?"

At last, Xu Shaoyu asked his wife to sell a piece of jade and two fur coats from their home. They got ninety silver coins. They then borrowed ten coins from others. Therefore, they returned the money on the due date. Several days later, Xu Shaoyu was completely cured. (from www.clearharmony.com)

I recommend that this story be taught in our public schools, private schools, church schools, and home schools, and be included in parental training.

One of the core values that my parents instilled in me when I was growing up was to always keep a promise. Our neighbors all lived by this code, because we were so very interdependent. As I learned after leaving the farm, not everyone grew up with that same core value. I still maintain keeping a promise at the top of my belief system, and I find unacceptable how so many people place so little importance on it.

# Drawbridge Mentality

Somewhere around our home we have a small carved wooden bowl and an unlabeled bottle of something that we assume is an alcoholic beverage of some kind. These two items were a gift to me from a woman whom I met under strange circumstances. I was involved with her for no more than ninety minutes, but those ninety minutes made an impact on my life.

In the early 1980s I made frequent business trips to New York City. I usually flew into Newark or LaGuardia Airport, but on one trip I flew for the first time into John F. Kennedy. A cab ride from Kennedy into the city cost a lot, so I rushed to board a Port Authority bus that was just about to pull away. As I stepped on I saw that one of the two front seats right by the door was vacant. I took it, thinking, *How convenient, I will be first off at the Port Authority Terminal and will not have the usual struggle to get a cab*. I sat down and immediately understood why that desirable seat was unused. Sitting in the window seat was a pathetic-looking woman who appeared to be a bag lady. She had a frayed, colorless scarf tied around her head and an old, worn, gray, faded long coat with the shoulder padding showing through. As I soon observed, she was wearing old, worn work shoes and was carrying a large brown-paper shopping bag. If that was not enough, she smelled of wood smoke as if she had been exposed to a wood-burning fireplace. I looked around with the intention of relocating, but my better judgment told me, *That woman, no matter her appearance, is a human being, and I will not hurt her feelings.*

The driver started walking through the bus collecting the fares. I was the first to pay, after which he spoke rudely to the woman beside me, demanding her money. It was obvious that she was totally lost and had no idea how to respond. After a bit of a commotion I pulled out the five-dollar fare and handed it to the driver. The driver scorned me saying, "Buddy, you just got screwed." We pulled away and headed for the city.

The woman touched my arm to get my attention and made a gesture that seemed to be saying "Thank you" while looking bewildered as if she suddenly realized what had just occurred. She started to pull things from her bag. First was a brown, document-sized envelope containing correspondence. After rummaging through the envelope she handed me a letter with what I took to be an address for some town in Romania. On the outside of the letter was a return address in New York City.

I knew that at that time Romania was one of the poorest countries in the world. I was by that time quite familiar with New York City and knew her destination address to be a street in the Hell's Kitchen area, one of the roughest spots in New York City. The woman, whom I now started to think of as "Mrs. Romania," took the letter and moved her finger along the words, stopping at a name. In a gesture that is universal mother language, she formed her arms into a cradling position and swung gently back and forth.

I used my best charade to ask, "Is that your son?"

Tears started to flow as she placed her weathered hands in a prayer position and placed them against the side of her head and closed her eyes. Soon after, she

pulled a small envelope from her bag and showed me a newspaper clipping. I choked up myself when I read the clipping, which told the news of a murder that had taken place in New York City. The name of the deceased man matched the name in the letter she had showed me. It was obvious by now that this poor mother was coming to New York to bury her son.

I started to think of what this poor grieving mother would do when we got to the Port Authority bus terminal. When we got off the bus, I made motions to communicate to her to watch for her baggage. There was none. Apparently, everything this woman had in America was in that bag. I gestured for her to follow me. Luckily, I hailed a cab right away. Once in the cab, I saw that we had a really fat Italian woman for our driver. I explained to the driver that we were to first deliver this woman, who was here from Romania, to the address that I had written down for her and then she was to take me across town to my business meeting. I told her that I would pay both cab fares when she dropped me off. The driver, seeing the clear difference between Mrs. Romania and me, inquired about our connection. I told her the story and she, like the bus driver, chided me and said I was a victim of a con woman.

We had made it only about four city blocks when I explained to the driver that I had plenty of small bills to pay what would have been the fare for my ride, but I needed change for a hundred-dollar bill to pay the additional fare for Mrs. Romania. Boy, did she explode!

"I don't have change for a G–d–n hundred-dollar bill!" She switched back and forth between cursing in Italian, English, and gibberish. The English words were sprinkled with f-words and g-d-words, adding that "these G–d–n people come here creating all kind of problems. They should be sent back or never allowed to come here in the first place!"

I could take it no longer, so I screamed at the top of my lungs, using a few expletives myself.

"Listen to me, woman. From your accent you haven't been long off the boat yourself, and I bet that someone helped you along the way! I see a precinct station right there, so stop this cab and we will discuss your legal status with the cops, and if you don't stop at one of these check-cashing stations so I can break this hundred-dollar bill, you won't get paid, and you will never be able to get out of the trouble that I will bring down on you!" She stopped, I got change, and we proceeded on with a very quiet cab driver.

I started to wonder, *Is Mrs. Romania really doing all this just to con me?* My skepticism was quieted when she pulled out a small, hand-carved wooden bowl with a matching lid and a bottle with no label. I tried everything to resist her giving me those things, knowing that they were meager treasures that she had brought to her family, but it was to no avail. She insisted on my having them. Mrs. Romania, with tear-filled eyes, said something in her language, and placed her hand on my shoulder, hesitating to hug me. I took her hand off my shoulder, slid close to her, and gave her a strong hug. She smiled a big, teary smile. It meant nothing to her, but I said, "We must stop meeting like this."

When we arrived at her address, I pointed to her building, which had the street name and building number displayed. Mrs. Romania stepped out of the cab and disappeared into the Hell's Kitchen crowd looking not so out of place.

I was thinking, *Now I have to ride in this cab in New York City with this irate Italian woman with no witness aboard.* I gave the driver my destination address.

She was quiet for a while, but finally broke the silence, saying in a gentle voice, "Mister, that was really nice what you did for that woman. I apologize for my anger. Yes, I have not been here so long myself."

I accept your apology and hope you learned something. *When you get to the Promised Land, don't pull up the drawbridge.*

# Faith that Won't Shake

In the early 1980s, I was involved in a fledgling company that I owned with my partners Davis Walker and Gene Wagester. We were struggling with 18% prime interest rates and an energy crisis-generated recession. Our business was engineering and construction of systems to convert companies that used large amounts of natural gas and/or oil to an alternative form of energy. We had our own systems for processing waste-combustible biomass to a fuel that could replace carbon-based fuels. The problem was that borrowing money was so expensive that companies were reluctant and slow to make decisions on new technology. We were in a position in which we were running out of money and sorely needed a new contract to survive. Gene, Davis, and I had already taken ourselves off salary in order to remain a viable company.

It was under these circumstances that I was traveling south through Georgia on my way to Tallahassee, Florida, in pursuit of business. It was under these circumstances that I met a most unforgettable man.

About one hundred miles north of the Florida line,

I stopped at a convenience store for a snack and a drink. As I was leaving the store, I was approached by a man who appeared to be in his forties. It was in mid-summer and dreadfully hot. He asked me where I was headed. I explained that I was headed south to Interstate 10 in Florida and from there heading west to Tallahassee. He said he was headed in the same direction toward Interstate 10, but from there would head east to his home in Florida. He asked if he could come along with me.

I have always been reluctant to pick up hitchhikers under any circumstances. I quickly evaluated the situation. He was very thin and was wearing only a tee shirt and light blue, denim jeans. His pockets looked flat, so I judged that there was no room for a weapon. I noticed that he had a sneaker on one foot and a cut off sandal on the other foot. After a quick review of things in my mind, I decided to give him a ride. He walked with a very bad limp and appeared to be in considerable pain with each step.

My situation and condition that day were quite different from my passenger's. I had on very expensive business attire—a fine suit with the jacket hanging in the back of my late model Mercury automobile that had a perfectly functioning air conditioner, a Rolex watch, fine shoes, and I had cash in my pocket along with credit cards with high limits. I had been driving alone for a long time and had worked myself into a state of depression over business conditions, the economy, and any other thing I could think of that brought discomfort to my soul and body. I was about as up-tight as anyone could make themselves.

This was unusual and scary for me. The reason I had stopped the car was to try and break my downbeat mood.

Once we were in the car, I felt that I would be more comfortable if I started a conversation with my passenger. I asked him about his foot, and he told me he had worked as a roofer but had fallen off a house and crushed his foot. He said the man he worked for had no health insurance or workmen's compensation coverage. He said his wife had lost her job when the textile plant in their town

closed down, and that there were no jobs available. With no money, he could not get the operation he needed on his foot. He continued talking, although I was drifting in and out of listening. I was thinking of my own problems. He explained that he had heard there were jobs in some town in Georgia, but when he got there the jobs were all gone. As we both loosened up, the conversation grew more relaxed. He talked of life and the many problems he had overcome. He spoke of his faith in God and that one should never give up hope.

I started to listen to him which took my mind off my own problems. I asked him how long he had been hitch-hiking. He answered that he had started out the day before. I asked if he had eaten that day. He said the last time he had eaten was the morning of the day before, and that meal had taken his last money. I pulled into the next store I saw and said, "Let's go in and get you something to eat."

"You don't have to do that, Mister," he said.

We went into the store and I told him to get anything he wanted. He got a quart of milk and a large box of Oreo cookies. Once back in the car, he thanked me over and over, drank all the milk, and ate half the cookies. He looked at me and said, "Mister, if you don't mind, I'm gonna keep the rest for later."

As we drove on, he talked about a variety of sub-jects—his wife, his family, his church, and his friends. I realized that he had a really wonderful attitude about life. He asked many questions about my own family, my life, and my career. I complimented him on his good attitude, considering the seemingly insurmountable problems he was facing. He said, "I have seen worse times, but things always work out for a man if he has faith and doesn't let things get him down."

I asked about his childhood, and he told me that he grew up during the Great Depression in a sharecropper's family. He said they often ran completely out of money and he and his five brothers and sisters were hired out to any farmer who needed help in their cottonfields. He said that oftentimes the only food they had was leftovers that the farmer they worked for would tell his wife to give them to take home. I am familiar with this because, as poor as my family was, we have been on the giving side of the same situation.

We shared stories of how drought years would leave very little money with which to survive the winter. We talked of gathering at the church to pray and collect for a family whose meager possessions had been burned up in a fire. He recalled as a youth that the family always looked to and sought strength in a small church that they attended. He looked at me with soulful eyes and said, "Well, you and I are still here doing fine, so I think that faith stuff works out mighty well."

The way he included me in the comment hit me in my soul. I had lived through those scenes that he spoke about. Listening to him reminded me of listening to a sermon or a speech that caused me to think of the things that really anchored my life, some of which I had drifted from. These can be bittersweet words. They are good for clarifying the important things in life, but can be painful for reminding you of how you have drifted from your core character. Once this thought settled on me, I realized that something important was happening in my life. This man's early life mirrored my own. In adulthood I had accomplished far more in material wealth, but it seemed as if he had held anchor better than I.

Somewhere north of Florida a strange, calm feeling descended on me and I had an epiphany. Here was this humble, simple man sitting beside me with very serious problems of his own, revealing things to me that changed my attitude towards my own problems. We discussed life in general. I have often reflected on that day when facing tough times. I can still repeat some of his conversation to myself. That experience helped change my life in a positive way. It wasn't that he eloquently explained life or that he made profound statements. It was his simple, non-questioning faith, expressed to me at a low point in my life, that has stuck with me until this day.

We got to the intersection of Interstate 10 in Florida. I pulled off and stopped on the ramp to let him out and wished him good luck. He thanked me several times and said, "You seemed a little tense yourself when I got in your car. Were you a little afraid of picking up a stranger, or were you a little worried about something yourself?"

Suddenly I thought, *What on earth do I have to worry about?*

I pulled away a couple of hundred feet or so and looked back. I had a strange feeling that he would fade away like some aberration that God had placed beside me to adjust my attitude. He was there alright, limping towards the next spot where he would stand and wait for another ride in an attempt to get home to his family. I couldn't leave that easily. I blew my horn and backed up. I got out of the car and he gave me a somewhat startled look. I took all the cash I had, about $140, and handed it to him. He took the money reluctantly. I said, "Just do this. Go to that motel and get a room for the night and have a couple of good meals before you go on."

"Have you talked to your family lately?" I asked.

"Last week," he replied

I gave him my telephone credit card number, explained how to use it, and told him to call his family. With a tear in his eye he asked, "Did God send you mister?"

I could only get out these words, "No sir. God sent you."

I believe God did have a hand in our meeting. I have often thought of that experience and how a poor, humble man with difficult circumstances of his own taught me some of the most important lessons of my life. *Don't let things get you down, do the best you can, and have faith that things will work out. They will!*

When I got my phone bill, two phone calls had been placed, one for thirty seconds and one for five minutes.

Our company did succeed, and things have never gotten me down again as badly as they had that day I met unforgettable John Doe.

# Taught to Share

I was raised in a home where we shared what we had. We were poor and had little money to share, so we shared what we acquired through our labor—namely food that we raised. Daddy always planted far more than our family could use ourselves, although we preserved, canned, salted, dried, and used it any other way to provide the fruits of our labor year-round. He would invite our city relatives and friends to pick freely from our gardens. Tending those gardens was hard work, and I readily admit to some resentment at seeing my cousins taking food from them, never having chopped a weed out or done any labor to help raise those fruits and vegetables. I wondered out loud to my daddy once, "Why don't they come out and help us with the work?" My dad shrugged his shoulders and said, "Some people just don't think that way. You share with folks because it's the right thing to do, and besides, it gives me joy."

Having been raised with the practice of giving and doing for others as a natural part of life, I never really considered how I would carry this practice with me as I moved into life on my own. For several years, particularly when I was in college years and in early married life, I had very little money to share. My sharing was limited to donating to the church and various charities. Simply giving money did not give me that feeling you get when you help someone directly. I started to rethink my personal attitude toward giving and sharing when I assumed responsibility for a large number of employees as a plant manager.

I was on a business trip to California when there was an airline strike that left people stranded worldwide, some for weeks. American Airlines was the only carrier to remain in service for one more day. I was to fly to Chicago on American, change to another airline that was on strike, and continue on to Greensboro, North Carolina. When I got to Chicago, I was stranded. People were trying every way possible to get home. Folks tried renting everything from cars and trucks to motorcycles. I talked to one man who was attempting to ship himself on a freight truck back to Texas. There seemed to be no hope. I overheard an airline employee, who was available to help us stranded passengers find a way home, announce, "If you are going south, there is a train heading south within the hour leaving from LaSalle Station. That word "south" sounded good to me, so with baggage in tow, I followed a group to LaSalle Station. Our group included a sailor, a soldier, a pregnant woman, and a young mother with an infant. As you might expect, the military guys took the baggage for the two women.

As we rushed up to the train, we were met by a porter

who shouted out, "Climb aboard; we will sell you a ticket later." We got on what could only be described as a cattle car with benches. I had cash only. (Credit cards were not available to me at that time.) After I paid for my ticket, I had twelve dollars left, but was thrilled to hear that the train was going to pass through Greensboro. As we pulled away from the station, I turned to the sailor sitting beside me and said, "It will probably take eight hours to get to Greensboro." The pregnant woman said, "Mister, I've done it before. It takes thirty-eight hours."

We soon discovered that there was no food service on board. Hour after boring hour we sat with no services. Eventually, we all started to complain to the porter, who rarely came through the car. Being the businessman and dressed in a good suit and tie, I told the porter that they had better make arrangements for food service soon or there would be payback. The conductor came through and announced that we were stopping in Richmond, Indiana, and that a woman was coming onboard with sandwiches and soft drinks. We did stop, and the woman went about selling sandwiches. I noticed that the mother with the baby did not buy any food. Her baby was becoming fretful and restless, so I went to her seat and asked if she had any money. She said no. "I was on Eastern and expected to be in Asheville by now," she explained. I then asked her if she had milk for her baby, and she again answered no. I told the porter who was assisting the food seller that he must hold the train until I ran to a small store that was visible in the distance and bought some milk for the baby. I think by now the porter thought I was a lawyer, so he did not argue. I got back on board with milk for the baby, and I insisted that the young mother take my sandwich. I realized as I gave her my sandwich that I was down to much less than enough for another one. I took my seat and tried to sleep, but was really too hungry. I finally slept until I needed to go the toilet. As I passed the young sleeping mother with the sleeping baby in her arms, I felt the same joy that my dad felt when friends and relatives picked from our garden.

We finally arrived in Greensboro at about midnight, where Lucille was there to meet me, and we had a joyous reunion. When I saw my children, LaVisa and Perry, my heart was overflowing.

I had just experienced a life-shaping event.

# What Is Love?

In the late 1960s Perry Harrison, at the time, the Chatham County School Superintendent, appointed me to serve on a biracial committee. I worked on the committee into the 1970s. The committee's purpose was to discuss problems and propose policies that would facilitate and assist in integrating the school system. Racial tension was present in Chatham County as it was everywhere in the South during those days, and the air in our meetings was thick with the probability of conflict. Very understandably, because of their varied backgrounds and life experiences, the members held different views on issues.

Part of our meeting structure, as proposed by Mr. Harrison, was to start each meeting with casual conversation. We were to bring up any subject we desired that constituted friendly chitchat before we discussed any contentious issues. Often just speaking up with light-hearted subjects would break the ice and set a friendly tone for the heavier part of our sessions.

Something happened at one of our meetings that has been heavy on my mind and in my heart ever since. It brought to my attention a situation that schoolteachers often see, but the rest of us barely notice.

One member of our committee was a black female special education teacher. At the beginning of one evening meeting, she asked if she could share something that happened in her class that day. The episode that the teacher described caused a permanent adjustment to my value system and views on life.

She went on to describe one of her white female students who was ten years old, very frail, and small for her age. She explained that the girl wore the same faded brown cotton dress for days at a time. Her hair was tangled and showed no sign of regular brushing. There was evidence of having been too long away from soap and water, and her attention span was short, causing her to doze off in class. The teacher admitted that she herself had choked up many times looking at this poor girl and wondering about her home life.

At that point, the teacher took from a folder a sheet of tablet paper that reminded me of the kind of paper I had used in my grammar-school days, grayish with broad spaces between the lines. Little chips of wood showed in the paper. Before passing it around for us to read, the teacher told us she had asked the class to write an answer to the question, "What is love?"

I was sitting beside her and was the first to accept the paper when she passed it around. The writing was large, scrawling print, written mostly outside the lines. When I read the words, I choked up. I could not speak, so I just

passed it along to the next member. On the paper, that little sad, neglected child had written these words: "I don't know what love is. When I got here it was gone."

As the paper was passed around and read, it left not a dry eye in the room.

Our meetings seemed to take on a more mellow and conciliatory tone from that point on. There seemed to be a bond between us after that, and there seemed to be more acceptance of each others' opinions and feelings.

My heart said to me, *If that black teacher could share that heartbreaking story with the emotion she expressed toward a neglected little white girl, maybe there could be grounds for reconciliation between the races after all.*

# Forgiving Ourselves

In the spring of 1966, our son Perry was near his third birthday, coming up on August 8. I was struggling with a blinding disease for which there was no treatment at the time. We were living in the first home that Lucille and I built in Goldston, North Carolina. I had recently purchased a used yard tractor with a forty-eight-inch cut. One day Perry and I were home alone, and I wanted to cut my grass. Because Perry wanted to be with me and under my feet constantly I had trained him to stay out of the yard when I mowed. I did this training by letting him sit in my lap for a drive around the yard. Once we had finished the round I would take him into the house and have him promise to stay in a room that was away from windows so that, if a rock were cast through the window by the mower, he would be safe.

On this day we were making that one round with Perry sitting in my lap, and I decided to engage the mower since all other times had been uneventful. Somewhere along the way—and this is where I totally lost all memory of what happened next—I suddenly found myself lifting the mower off Perry. I somehow flipped the tractor and mower upside down and lifted Perry into my arms. Perry was losing blood rapidly. At the time, I drove a company pickup truck, a 1963 six-cylinder, dark green Chevrolet. You may wonder why I remember these details or mention them now. It is because of the way I came to despise that truck. There was a bloodstain on the vinyl seat back that never went away, and I saw it every time I got in that truck.

I bundled Perry in my arms and rushed to my truck. I had my left arm around his body, holding together a bloody face and a battered and cut-up arm and hand.

I don't remember much after that, except that I drove as fast as that truck would go on my way to the hospital in Sanford, North Carolina. I slowed down only for red lights.

The trip to the hospital is a blur. I do remember that I heard a most beautiful sound at the first stoplight in Sanford by what was then a Holiday Inn. Perry whimpered. Thank God Perry whimpered. I made it to the emergency entrance to the hospital and went running and screaming into the hospital with what I thought to be my dying son nestled in my arms. I met Dr. Oelrich, a prominent Sanford surgeon. I was screaming, "Help me, help me!" Nurses came from all over. My left hand was stuck to Perry from the clotted and crusted blood. Dr. Oelrich and the nurses had to carefully separate my fingers and hand from Perry, who was quiet and motionless. Once I was cleared from Perry, they laid him on an operating table and started to work on him. I completely lost control. I

begged them to take my life so Perry could live. I would not take no for an answer because, in my mental condition, I truly believed that my dying would save Perry. Dr. Oelrich had the nurses give me a shot to calm me down.

It took 250 stitches to put our two-and-a-half-year-old son together. I stayed in the hospital with Perry most of the two weeks while he was there. One night I overheard Perry mumbling. I jumped up, spoke to him, and kissed his forehead.

Perry said, "Hush, Daddy! I am saying my prayers."

"I understand, Perry. I don't stop praying."

That first night, the nightmares started. I would awaken sweating and in a panic. I tried to hide this from the family. I cried alone a lot. The guilt would not let up. People would ask me about the accident, and I thought I could see in their eyes and in their voices an accusing tone.

At the time I worked as assistant plant manager. My boss lived in Siler City, North Carolina. He would give me reports of what people were saying. He may have thought it was helping me to hear the cold, vicious things people said about me—that I was a bad parent, that I was stupid and careless were some of the vilest comments. What made these comments so painful was the fact that I agreed with all of them. If it had not been for my faith and Lucille's love and support, I may have gone crazy.

Perry has some permanent damage, which is always a reminder of that horrible day in 1966, but he grew into a warm, loving, and lovable man for whom I would still give my life.

Another anxiety set in on me after the accident: *How could I ever discipline my son?* Every child needs strong parental guidance, but how could I look at Perry and not see the scarred eye, scarred arm, scarred hand, and be firm with him? That concern never materialized. Perry was such a joy to raise that strong discipline was never necessary. Given my own mischievous background I would witness Perry's little naughty acts and could only think, *That's my boy!*

Two situations when Perry required a little talking-to stand out in my memory. One time, in about the fifth grade, he called a little black girl the b-word because she had called him a "honky." For this he was sent home. For our part, Lucille and I decided that a little more punishment was due. We cut him off TV for a week. He begged to just sit in the den while we watched the family shows. We agreed, but with one caveat: He would have to sit with his back to the TV. One night, as we were watching a show, Perry laughed at a time when he would have to have seen the scene to know it was funny. I gave a good look his way and saw that he had positioned himself so he could watch TV in the reflection from the French doors. He was missing nothing. I thought to myself, *That's my boy!* Who could have stopped him from that?

Another time, I was going to mow the yard and needed my gas can filled. I gave Perry two dollars and told him to take the empty can to the service station about a tenth of a mile from our home. The two dollars was enough money to fill the can and leave about twenty-five cents. I told Perry he could buy candy with the remainder of the money. Perry returned with the can filled and a large bag of candy. I asked him how he had bought so much candy.

He said, "You told me I could spend the leftover money for candy."

I asked him how much money was left after filling the can.

Perry said, "Two dollars."

"How did you pay for the gas and have two dollars left over?"

He very sheepishly said, "I charged the gas." I had to say to myself, *That's my boy!*

When Perry was about eight years old, he went with me to Sanford, driving that same route we had taken to the hospital that fateful day. As we passed the Holiday Inn, Perry looked up and said, "Daddy, I remember seeing those wires the day you took me to the hospital." We had been at that very spot when I had heard that wonderful *I-am-still-alive* whimper come from him.

Time eventually healed most of the pain, but I still find it tough to revisit that horrible scene even to this day, and whether I have ever forgiven myself is still an open question. To Perry's credit, he has never said or done the slightest thing to hint at blaming me or making me feel guilty.

I have posed this question more than once to my Sunday school class: *Is there someone you would willingly die for?* The standard answer is that, yes, they would die for their children, which provokes an interesting discussion about responsibility to the ones left behind. It is often the case that the question is then turned back on me, and my answer is always an emphatic "yes"—and for good reason. I have been tested.

# Beating the Odds

About two years ago I was watching TV when the phone rang. The voice on the other end asked, "Is this LaVerne Thornton?" Of course, I answered in the affirmative. Then came these words: "This is Ricci Stroud." I was almost shocked. Ricci Stroud is my mother's first cousin, making me his first cousin once removed. I said, "Let's not say another word until we decide how long it's been since we've heard from each other." The math took a while. I was seventy-three at the time, and Ricci was seventy. We had seen neither hide nor hair of each other, and had not even spoken or corresponded in more than fifty-five years. I didn't know if Ricci was calling from prison, an old folks' home, or perhaps he was being held by the CIA in a secure location somewhere. You see, the last time I had seen Ricci, he and my sisters and I had been on the farm working in a tobacco field. We had called him "The Dreamer." My sister declares that one day he was staring into space and threw a tobacco sucker that hit her in the mouth. What had brought Ricci to the farm was an attempt to put some order and stability into his life through hard work and discipline, but that didn't seem to be taking place. He stopped helping us on the farm when I was about fifteen years old, and I never heard from Ricci again until that night with the phone call.

Ricci's problems centered on family difficulties. His nine-year-old brother Homer was killed by a train while walking home from school. Homer's death practically destroyed his mother. She spent some time being treated at Duke Hospital in Durham, North Carolina for a mental breakdown. All this had placed a heavy burden on little twelve-year-old Ricci. I don't know many details about that period of Ricci's life, because I went off to school at Virginia Tech and lost contact with a lot of life back home. I heard that Ricci had left home when I was eighteen, which would have made him fifteen years old.

At the end of my and Ricci's phone call, we set a date for me to visit him in Danville, Virginia. By that time, he had purchased around eighty copies of my first book, *Walk in 'e Moon*, most of which he had given away. We met in a restaurant for breakfast on the day of my visit. Ricci appeared to know everyone in the place, and they all treated him as a good friend. I was introduced as the man who wrote "the book." After breakfast, I followed Ricci to his beautiful home, which was built on the most beautiful, rolling hills. I dropped my truck off, and rode with him through a lovely area north of Danville. We toured a farm owned by Ricci where there was a cabin that is more than 250 years old. He had restored it to perfection.

Renewing our relationship was a totally warm and

friendly experience, and it seemed that no time or space stood between the present and the last time we had seen each other so many years ago. Of course, neither of us had escaped the ravages of time. We are both old and gray now. As we rode and talked, we discovered a real affection for each other. From all appearances, Ricci was successful both materially and spiritually—a man of faith surrounded by an abundance of friends. My curiosity was piqued as I wondered aloud how Ricci had arrived at such an accomplished position in life with obstacles so stacked against him.

Ricci very matter-of-factly told me his story. He had, in fact, left home at fifteen years old and, from that day on, lived on his own. He picked up a simple, low-paying job delivering groceries. The work barely sustained him, so he would go to one of the Dan River Mills parking lots as the third shift was coming on, watch for people to leave their cars, and then try the doors until he found a car that was left unlocked. That car would be his bedroom for the night. In the morning, he would go to a local service station and clean up. Ricci met his wife Linda in a soda shop in 1957 when he was seventeen and Linda was fifteen. They were married two years later. At the time neither had finished high school. They struggled to get Linda through graduation. When they were first married, they lived in a small, run-down home on North Main Street in Danville, Virginia that they shared with an elderly couple for four years until their son Jeff was born. Jeff's birth brought on new problems, namely a need for space and more money to raise their son. At the time of Jeff's birth, Ricci was working at a bottom-line job at Dan River Mills that was disappearing. Things looked bleak for the couple.

Ricci drove me to a spot across the street from the home he and Linda shared with their elderly friends. We parked and Ricci told me this story;

"When Jeff was born, I was concerned about how to feed my family. I was standing at this spot at 11:30 one night waiting for a bus to take me to my job at Dan River Mills. I looked at the moon shining through that stark, leafless oak tree and started to pray. I asked God to please help me find work that would pay me enough money to support my family. I told God that I would serve him and be faithful to him for the rest of my life if I could find a way to support my wife and newborn baby. In less than two weeks I was offered a dairy route with Sealtest Dairy making enough money to take care of Linda and Jeff. The man who gave me that wonderful opportunity is J. W. Wilkinson. I love that man to this day and still maintain a close friendship with him. I have, as best I could, kept my promise to God."

Later that day, Ricci took me to meet Mr. Wilkinson. and gave him a Christmas gift and a signed copy of my book. We traded stories for a while. I could see a loving connection between the two of them and a need to share a quiet moment, so I went outside and waited for Ricci. He came out wiping his eyes and said, "I love that man. I owe him so much."

His new job allowed Ricci and Linda to buy a small home. Soon he was handling his dairy route in far less than eight hours and had saved enough money to buy a used mobile home that he rented out. The lot was large enough to add two more rental mobile homes. One rental unit at a time, Ricci built a substantial residential rental business.

Ricci's life is a simple lesson for all whiners and people who give in and give up. The financial success Ricci has had is really nothing spectacular, but beating the odds to accomplish what he has in life is quite extraordinary. Accomplishing this while maintaining faith, dignity, style, and grace is, in fact, spectacular.

When I got home that night, Lucille asked me how it had gone. I answered her with words I use to bestow my highest award on a new friend, "Honestly sweetheart, it was love at first sight."

*Here's to you my friend. Staring into space and dreaming paid off for you. I am proud to be your cousin.*

# Helping Dave Die

Dave Watson knew for more than a year that he was dying. The last year of his life was one of the most intense experiences in human relationships I have ever had. He was suffering with terminal esophageal cancer, and I spent that year helping Dave ease the pain of facing death.

When he told me the doctors did not recommend any treatment, and that his condition was terminal, I immediately told Dave I would be with him, loving and supporting him until the end. I never considered how many ways this commitment would affect my life. Dave and I had developed the kind of relationship which gave him the confidence that my promise was sincere. I considered it my duty to help my dear friend die with dignity.

Dave and I kept up our regular walking program at Kiwanis Park in Sanford, North Carolina, until he started to stumble a bit. Being the kind of man he was, Dave would not suggest changing the routine that had become such an important part of our lives. I had heard that First Presbyterian Church in town had an indoor walking track, and they welcomed non–church members to use it.

I suggested that Dave and I give it a visit. We tried out the track, liked it, and moved our routine to the church. I could see an immediate improvement in Dave's steps. As his pace grew slower, Dave would frequently complain that he was slowing me down. I had to constantly remind him that he was my priority. He always put others first, but he accepted my position and confessed to me how

important it was for me to be with him on our daily routine. Eventually we had to shorten our distance and slow our pace.

A few months before he died, Dave had to give up driving, so I would pick him up and take him to the church. We soon had to use the elevator to get up to the track. By then Dave was using a walker, and while we still took our walk, it was becoming very difficult for him. We often took a very long, circuitous route back home, just cruising around. Dave loved those rides and would always say they were the highlight of his days. Even when he could no longer walk the track I would pick him up and take him to the church to meet and have coffee in the church library with some of the people we had met there. All greeted Dave with loving warmth and concern. Folks were impressed with how he never gave up and always wore a big smile. After leaving the church, and before Dave got too sick to go out at all, I would take him for a drive through the countryside. We would often have to stop for him to throw up, but we still drove around several days a week until he became bedridden.

On one drive we were in a remote area of Chatham County and Dave suddenly said, "Looks like wild turkeys." I stopped the car, and sure enough, in the distance there was a group of wild turkeys. We sat quietly with the engine shut off and just watched as the turkeys pecked through the field until they got to the narrow, paved road. They slowly strutted across the road and disappeared into the woods. I commented to Dave that he had really good eyesight, and if he had not been with me, I would have surely missed those turkeys and would not have enjoyed those minutes of a truly beautiful, natural scene.

Dave looked at me and said, "I have always had good eyes. Facing death has not improved my eyesight, but it sure has improved my vision and appreciation for what I see."

From that moment on, I vowed that, when with Dave, I would start seeing things as if I didn't have long to live and was perhaps seeing them for the last time. God's creation looked a little clearer. Funny thing, my usually impatient self never surfaced when I was on those little excursions with Dave.

Dave and I would talk about any subject: What it is like to know that you are dying, what love of family and friends means, and how he had no fear. On numerous occasions Dave told me, "This has been the best year of my life."

One day when he was still getting out some, he said, "I know that people mean well, but I just get exhausted when they stay so long." I suggested that he have a "Please limit your visit" sign put on the door. Even though the sign was put up, some people didn't comply.

Dave told me a story that really made me smile. Dave would never say a disparaging word about anyone, so I was amused when he told me, "So-and-so came over yesterday and stayed almost two hours," adding, "I didn't like him real good when I was well." That was the worst thing that Dave Watson ever said to me about anyone.

Every time I saw Dave after that sign went up, he would say, "Now that sign does not apply to you." So

near the end, I did sit and hold his hand for a while, but shortened my visits.

Another time, Dave told me that his family insisted he must eat to keep his strength up, but that he could not stand the taste of food and that mealtime was his worst time of the day. I suggested that he discuss it with his hospice nurse. The next morning, Dave said, with a broad smile, "I don't have to eat unless I want to."

The last time I saw Dave, I hugged his wasted body, kissed his forehead, and told him that I loved him. Dave said in an almost inaudible voice, "I love you, too, LaVerne. You have been one of the best things that ever happened in my life." In typical Dave fashion, he added, "You have been too good to me."

*So have you, Dave. So have you.*

Being with Dave Watson in his last year, and watching him die with such dignity, didn't improve my eyesight, but it really has improved my vision and appreciation for what I see.

# Encouragement

When I was in the sixth grade, my teacher, Mrs. Heinz, took a special interest in me. One day during recess, I was shooting marbles (one of my best skills) and winning. Mrs. Heinz walked up, reached down, and took me by the hand, saying, "LaVerne, go for a walk with me." She held my hand, and we walked the entire perimeter of the school grounds. How embarrassing was that? I could see everyone looking and whispering, "Pee Wee is the teacher's pet." What Mrs. Heinz was doing during our walk was telling me how intelligent I was, and how I could become anything I wanted to if I would apply myself. Boy, did I catch it at lunchtime! I told my classmates that Mrs. Heinz was explaining to me that if I didn't change—straighten up and fly right—that I was headed for reform school. Suddenly, with that little white lie, I turned the incident around and became a hero, but I felt really guilty for a long time.

Many times over the ensuing years, I carried a subliminal thought of Mrs. Heinz's words. I truly believe that her encouragement had an impact on my life. I am seventy-five years old as I write this. I am almost shock-proof, hard to impress, and I find fewer and fewer experiences life-altering. I want not to be misunderstood here, because I still love life, have lots of fun, and am told by those close to me that I am still quick-witted and alert. But the greatest impression made on me in the last few years was made by a child whom I believed to possess something special, and my relationship with him has been a most rewarding experience.

As the years piled up on me, I joined the old-fogey crowd, condemning the youth of today as a lost generation committed to iPods and avoiding responsibility. My image of our youth was changed several years ago when a handsome young family started attending Goldston United Methodist Church. One Sunday, their little son tugged on my sleeve and asked, "Do you want me to tell you a joke?" I replied yes, and he told me a funny joke that I wish I could remember. The next Sunday, I told him a joke and asked him to tell me one. There was something special about that kid that compelled me to say something to him. I really don't know where it came from, but it was sincere and I said it with conviction. "Young man, I have an unusual talent. I can look in young people's eyes and determine if they will be successful in life." I added, "I have never been wrong, and I know that you will be very successful in all respects and endeavors." I took out my little vial of nitro tabs that I carry because of a serious heart problem and declared, "But just in case you get out of line, I carry this nuclear-grade whup-ass that I can call up at a moment's notice." He understood the humor and got a kick out of it.

Ever since that day, Jason Buchanan the younger has been my friend. I have seen him mature, physically and intellectually, into an eighteen-year-old man who can comfortably discuss philosophy, religion, and politics with any adult. I have seen him lose wrestling contests only to strengthen his body and his mental resolve to become a winner the next time. The last time we talked, Jason said that people tell him to avoid politics and religion in conversations with others. Jason declared that most conversations other than politics and religion are mostly small talk. That is a profound thought, and it is pure Jason.

Jason Buchanan is my friend; the interesting thing is that he probably doesn't understand just how much he

has given me, not the least of which is the conviction that if a fraction of our youth is like Jason Buchanan, we as a people will be just fine.

*Thank you, my little buddy. I love you and believe in you. In fact, I have so much confidence in you that I am not going to renew my license to carry nuclear-grade whup-ass.*

NOTE: On Sunday, September 23, 2012 Jason was awarded the title of Eagle Scout, the highest rank attainable in the Boys Scouts of America.

# Friendship Born
# of Forgiveness

I love my Sunday school class. We are old, mostly wise, and have all been there, done that. One Sunday morning we were discussing forgiveness and the fact that, if you forgive someone but never forget the event that precipitated the need for forgiveness, you have really never forgiven them.

I took a different position. My position was that the wonderful feeling you get when you forgive or are forgiven should linger in your heart and soul forever. This experience should be there to call upon every time forgiveness is requested of you or asked by you. Such an experience occurred between me and someone who became one of my dearest friends. I will not use real names.

I also will not reveal the circumstances here because they do not matter. I will only say that it was in the mid-1960s, and that I remember the pain we each admitted to suffering. In less than a week after the incident we met, and immediately without saying a word, we embraced in a warm, friendly hug that soon brought these words, "I

am so sorry! Please forgive me. I want your friendship."
Thus was born a lifelong friendship between Betty, Bob,
Lucille, and me.

The four of us have for many years been a part of
each others' families. We have been on plane trips and
car trips and cruise ships. Our most recent trip was for
eight days. On that trip we shared every meal from the
first Saturday's lunch through the following Saturday's
dinner without conflict or dispute. It takes a strong
friendship to do that.

The great joy of traveling together is the wives' little-
girl excitement at everything we do. On a trip, those girls
awaken to a new world every day. They do tend to stay up
too late for us menfolk, though. One night on a cruise, we
boys were in bed and heard the girls come to our cabins
laughing hysterically.

The next morning, Bob and I were up early having
breakfast. I said to Bob, "What we heard last night is the
future: Our having passed on, and our wives traveling
the world giggling and acting as if we never existed." We
dropped the subject.

We four are getting old and often reflect back over
the years that we have shared friendship, joy, and pain.
Lucille and I feel as warm and accepted in their home as
we do in our own home. We encourage each other when
we suffer the problems that come with growing old, often
with humor and fun.

Two women brighten my life when they enter my
space. Lucille is first; Betty is a close second. There is only

one man with the talent and skills to keep me grounded: My friend Bob.

I often think, *What a joyous friendship we would have missed if sincere forgiveness had not been offered and accepted. I hope I never forget what happened to teach me that lesson.*

# A Moment

When I was in the fourth and fifth grades I fell in love with Nancy Cross. Although we had been in class together, the first time that I really, really noticed her, I suddenly felt that *I-am-in-love* feeling. Nancy was the brightest person in our class, and I was sort of intimidated by her brains. I remember cutting back on my devilment and working hard on my schooling so that I could impress her.

Nancy did not live in the isolated area of Virginia called the Bend, where I did. She lived in sight of the Happy Home School on the North Carolina side of the Virginia–North Carolina border, where I attended grammar school.

At the fifth-grade Christmas season I wanted to give Nancy a Christmas present. We were very poor, and I didn't want my parents to know that I was in love, so I asked Granny Pruitt to help me. The only thing we had to give Nancy was a bag of hard candy, in what was then called a cellophane bag. It was kept over from the past Christmas so that Granny could offer a little treat to whatever kid came around. She would always keep a fancy crystal bowl containing a few hard candies. Those were the "hard-candy Christmases" that Dolly Parton sings about. To let me take her whole bag to give to Nancy was a real sacrifice for Granny.

Our son, Perry, can tell you all about crystal bowls filled with melted hard candy. Perry says that every home he visited had a crystal bowl containing old hard candy. He says that all the flavors blend together in those bowls.

When I proudly presented my gift of hard candy melted into one big glob to Nancy, I could tell that she was not impressed. My heart sank.

I never knew whether Nancy loved me. Not to worry, though. I loved her enough for both of us.

When I first started liking Nancy I was challenged by the meanest, toughest boy in our class. Clegg (not his real name, because he is still alive and still mean) was one of those boys who attended school just to make it to sixteen so he could legally quit. He was shaving in the fifth grade. Clegg offered me a Red Ryder "thick book" in exchange for my giving up Nancy. That book had pictures in the top right corner of each page showing Little Beaver. The pictures were drawn like cartoons. You could take your thumb and flip the pages very fast, causing Little Beaver to run, jump on his pony, and shoot his bow. That book was a real treasure if ever there was one. My love for Nancy was so huge that I did not give up, even under the threat of Clegg beating me to death.

Nancy and I remained friends all through school but

never dated. We are photographed standing side by side in the school yearbook, having been voted Most Original by our classmates. My hormones flared after meeting Lucille Baker, and from that moment on, all other girls were for naught in the romance area.

We all graduated in 1955 and went our separate ways, except Lucille and I. We journeyed into a great life together.

Nancy became an English teacher and finished up her teaching career in South Boston, Virginia. Nancy and her husband, John, always attended our class reunions. I would kid her husband by saying such things as, "You can't possibly love Nancy any more than I did when we were ten and eleven years old."

Nancy did not attend our last class reunion, held in May 2011. We all wondered at her absence. Jimmy Pruitt, a mutual friend of Nancy's brother Bob's and mine, forwarded an email to me that he had received from Bob:

> Hazel and I visited with John and Nancy on Wednesday, prior to Mother's Day. We had a good visit but noticed that John can not speak too well and Nancy cannot remember that well. Nancy could not remember that we had been there when her son came home for Mother's Day.
>
> This past Thursday night, Lin, Nancy's son, called and said he was on the way to South Boston as John was in the hospital. I left at 6:00 AM on Friday and drove to the

hospital. When I got there and talked with Lin, he stated that John had a piece of meat stuck in his throat and could not swallow it. They did a procedure and removed it.

The doctor came in and talked with us after the procedure. He said that John was very weak and would continue to get weaker. He said that what we saw at that time was the best we would see John. John has acute lung cancer and according to this doctor, nothing can be done for him. Lin told the doctor that John had an appointment at Duke University hospital in Durham, NC on the 24th. The doctor said he could take him but he would not put him through the agony of the 1½ hour ride to Durham and then back. He advised that we take him home and make him as comfortable as possible. The doctor does not want him to travel.

John came home from the hospital last night. He can get around a little using a walker but is subject to fall at any time. This morning when we got up I noticed Nancy getting dressed a little more than if she was going to be at home. She came downstairs and I asked her where she was going. She told me she would ride with me if it was okay. Again, I asked her where we were going. She said, "We have got to go over there." Again I asked her where. She finally said we have to go to the hospital. I told her that John was home and we did not have to go to the hospital. She agreed that we didn't need to go.

So, from what I've written above, you can tell they will not be at the reunion. Normally Nancy tells me when your class is having a reunion. I saw an envelope from you but she did not mention anything about your reunion and I did not ask any questions. I will do my best to keep you informed.

Thanks for your concern.

Bob

After this email, I communicated with Bob directly. On Friday, December 9, at 8:30 p.m., I read this email from Bob:

> I gotta tell you, Nancy had shelves full of books in her house as she loved to read. When we moved her to her assisted living quarters, she chose three of her books to take with her. Your book, *Walk in 'e Moon*, was one of the three. As for the ones left back, she said, "Get rid of them."

I was very deeply moved by Bob's email.

I choked up a bit as I recalled the events that had occurred through the years that brought me to this moment.

Bob is going to visit Nancy during the Christmas holidays and read this story to her and ask her permission to include it in my book.

### EPILOGUE

I received this email from Bob:

> Nancy and I had a good visit yesterday.
>
> She looked better than I've seen her in some time. We talked and then took a walk around the facility.
>
> I talked with her about your upcoming book and read your story to her. My only wish is that you could have seen the smile on

her face. When I asked her if it was okay for you to publish this, she replied (with a huge smile), "If he feels he would like to write that story, I have no problem with it." She was very pleased that you wanted to do this.
Bob


After reading my book, *Walk in 'e Moon*, Bob Cross sent me a check along with Nancy's address and asked me to send her a copy.

I haven't had a chance to speak with her since she received my book

Nancy, I wish I had told you this story!

# Frozen Music

For years I have contemplated the disconnect between those people who are totally into the arts and those who are totally into the hardware side of life. Those people totally into the arts don't seem to understand those who don't care at all about classical music, plays, paintings, and so on. Those who are totally into the hardware side of life love country music, NASCAR, sports, and so on. They generally love to make things and construct stuff. Of course, there also are we people who are not totally enthused about either, but are semipassionate or lukewarm on them all.

In the mid-1970s I was at a party in New York City with my friend Ted. A woman there was, shall we say, avant-garde in every way. She could not leave me alone. She was one of those people who had to put southerners down. At one point she looked at me and said, "The South is dying. There is absolutely no culture there. I could never live without my cultural life!"

I was taken aback a bit, but said in my best southern drawl, "It's sorta hard to live without taters, too, you know," as the entire party listened in.

A point to be made here: Yankees listen to a southerner every time they speak, not for what they are saying, but for the way they are saying it. I have used that knowledge many, many times to my advantage. When I speak in a Yankee environment, I always get the floor.

So I said emphatically, "Listen, ma'am, you could destroy every painting, every piece of music, every play, and even the Bible, and life would move seamlessly along. Folks would get together and reproduce it all, but if you stop the trucks and trains from coming into New York for one month, you people would starve to death. Now you tell me, would a starving person prefer someone to read Plato to them or would they rather have a loaf of bread?" There was silence in the room.

Don't misunderstand me. I certainly am not opposed to the arts. I believe the arts enrich our lives. But taters keep us alive.

One night I was relaxing in the condominium I had in Pittsburgh when I got a phone call from a stranger. That was rare, because most of the time I only received calls from Lucille and my two business partners. The lady on the phone was soliciting donations for the Pittsburgh Symphony. I tried to explain to her that I was a part-time resident and that her cause was not on my donation list. She persisted to the point that I became irritated.

Finally she said, "Mister Thornton, if we don't support the arts, they will just die."

I thought, *You snob!*

I pulled up my best southern drawl and said, "Ma'am,

if your band was as good as Willie Nelson's, you wouldn't have to beg for money."

She hung up, but she had a story to tell. Do you think if we all talked that way, they would stop coming south?

These things lingered in my mind for years until they came forward when I started writing. Then a very important episode came to my mind.

Gene Wagester, Davis Walker, and I owned an engineering and construction company during the 1980s. One of the things we did was turnkey design and construction of animal feed production facilities. One of the processes we used was the slip-form concrete method, whereby a building is constructed by a continuous pouring of concrete. To build a feed mill would take us an average of thirty days—twenty-four hours a day, seven days a week—to completion.

Every year we had a booth at the annual southeastern egg and poultry show in Atlanta, which had the largest attendance numbers of any show held there. One year we prepared a stop-frame slideshow of the Cuddy feed mill being built. The film was timed to compress the thirty days into a start-to-finish time of eight hours. Every morning, we would start the show over again from the beginning. A huge number of people would check by regularly to see the progress. As you watched the slide show, you could see a rhythm going on. People were doing routine work while a slideshow of tasks was being performed. A supervisor was shown looking at prints as if he were reading the bars of music and waving his arms as if he were conducting.

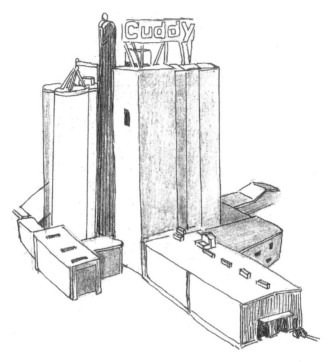

One guest came through several times every day to watch the show. He asked me once, "When does the show stop?" I told him that the mill would be complete at about five o'clock. He came around a few minutes before five to see the completion. As the final frame ran he looked at me and said, "I love music and going to the symphony. I have watched this all week, and have come to the conclusion that watching this structure go up has been like watching a symphony. Seeing it complete, and having watched it going up, I feel now as if I am looking at frozen music."

Lucille and I recently watched a film of the Gateway Arch in St. Louis being built. The Atlanta experience came back to me. We were looking at frozen music. Consider any major structure—a bridge, a skyscraper, or a dam—and imagine all the design, planning, and development that went into constructing it, and you have to conclude that art and hardware must have come together.

# Flowers for Dave

*Dave Watson was my best friend for twenty-one years. I wrote this for Dave and his family about six months before he died in April 2010. I will be forever grateful that Dave knew my feelings about him while he was alive.*

When I was growing up I often heard the old Carter Family song that includes the lyrics, "Give me the roses while I live, trying to cheer me on. Useless are flowers that you give after the soul is gone." I was captivated by those words as a child, but it took me until late in life to understand their full meaning. Dave Watson taught me the meaning and the lesson in those words.

I met Dave in early June 1989. I had just gotten out of a contract with a company that bought out my partners and me, and I was determined to improve my health with a regular walking program. The Kiwanis Park in Sanford, with its measured-mile track with flats and hills, was the ideal place to start. As I was walking one day I happened upon Dave Watson, and we started to walk along together. Neither one of us mentioned anything about walking regularly together; it just evolved that way. I would get to the park and Dave would already be there, or Dave would get to the park and I would be there. We walked and talked, and a routine developed. Soon we made an agreement that walking was more enjoyable if we had someone to walk with. Thus began a lifelong, life-altering relationship. We have walked and talked together for more than twenty years. We started to keep a record of our miles, and as of June 2009 we had walked the equivalent of going all the way to California and back twice—some thirteen thousand miles.

One day after I had met Dave, I told Lucille, "I met the nicest old man at the park." Dave was sixty-one at the time. I was a kid of fifty-two. I had a full beard then. I'm not a handsome man, but I was not flattered when Dave said he told his wife, Mary, that he had met a man at the park who looked just like Pappy Yokem.

During the ten years before I met Dave, I had traveled constantly on business. I would often spend a full week never seeing a single human being I had ever met before. I dealt with tough-minded businessmen in my work, and perhaps had become a bit jaded. My life had long since lost any semblance of being routine. Settling into a routine of walking five mornings a week with Dave seemed foreign to my nature, but I soon adopted Dave's uncomplicated philosophy of taking life as it comes and moving on. Now I need and want tradition and routine, and I appreciate the value of simple pleasures like watching for the blooming of the blackberries along our trail or waiting for the fall colors and the first frost of the season.

Spending an hour or so, five days a week, for over twenty years with a person generates a lot of memories. Dave and I have shared the good and bad times, but the good always overshadowed the bad.

Dave was diagnosed with prostate cancer in 1997 and subsequently had his prostate surgically removed. I wrote this poem and gave it to him before his surgery:

> Old friend,
> we have walked together
> through green valleys
> and
> by clear, running brooks.
> We have
> ascended mountains together.
> I was the talker.
> I rambled on and on.
> You,
> in the words of the poet,
> took my words,
> chaff and grain together,
> sifted them,
> kept what was worth keeping,
> and,
> with a kindly breath,

blew the rest away.
Now you are in a valley.
If you must walk
in the valley
of the shadow
of death,
you will not
walk alone

I hope and believe that I was there and suffered alongside Dave. He survived with courage and a strong faith in God. Then came my own longtime problem of facing blindness. Dave was always there with prayers and loving support as I received six of the twelve surgeries I have undergone to restore my vision. Dave and I, along with Leland Jackson—a great guy who joined us along the way—used to joke that, if I were to go blind, I would buy a used limo and hire a chauffer to drive us around. Every time I got my notice to renew my driver's license, Leland would ask, "If you don't pass, do we get our limo?" When I would meet Dave and Leland at the park the morning after getting a good eye doctor's report, Leland would say, "Dang, there goes our limo."

Then came heart surgery for me. Dave gave me great support and encouraged me to keep walking, and soon we were back to our full schedule.

We lost Leland to cancer in 2007. He was diagnosed on a Wednesday and died the following Saturday. Dave and I were with him two days before he died. We hugged Leland, and our last words to him were, "I love you, Leland."

Dave and I continued walking, grieving, and sharing Leland stories, and even today we recall our memories of the good times together with Leland.

We raised our grandchildren together and kept each other updated on our beloved families. I believe the aspects of our lives that we have not shared with each other over those twenty-odd years would make up a very short list.

It's funny what you think about when you reflect on a longtime relationship with another human being. I remember the time Dave and I went hiking in the Uwharrie Mountains in our brand-new, GORE-TEX-lined boots. The boots were supposed to be waterproof, so to test them out, we sat on a log that formed a bridge over a small creek. We ate our lunch with our feet submerged in the creek, and sure enough, the GORE-TEX-lined boots kept our feet dry. Birds were flying around while little fishes swam about. The sky was cornflower blue. Everything at the moment was right in our world.

And I remember the time Dave, Leland, and I climbed up to Hanging Rock—a really difficult hike. Exhausted, we looked at each other and said, almost in unison, "Enjoy the scenery, boys; we ain't ever gonna do this again!"

Then there were our apple-shopping trips to the mountains. We would take a fall trip to the mountains to buy fresh "mountain" apples from an apple orchard. On one trip, we were having so much fun that, when we were

almost home, one of us exclaimed, "We don't have any apples!" We stopped at a food market and bought some so we wouldn't have to explain to our families why we hadn't brought them any real "mountain" apples.

There were other big, significant events that have happened during our years of friendship, but the little ones stand out.

*This is a personal word to Dave:*

Dave, you are a wonderful friend. To have spent so much time with you has made me a better man and caused me to walk closer to God. I cannot think of a higher compliment, or it would be written here. Now, my old friend, you have been given a really steep mountain to climb. I will climb alongside you as long as I can. If you must go on alone, I will watch you cross the horizon into the waiting arms of God. Part of my life will be lived for you while you are here. If you leave me behind, part of me will go with you.

I love you, old friend. Enjoy these flowers.